T0129901

# Becoming

A Journey Toward Wholeness

Alexandra Grayson

authorHOUSE®

*AuthorHouse*™
*1663 Liberty Drive*
*Bloomington, IN 47403*
*www.authorhouse.com*
*Phone: 1 (800) 839-8640*

*Published by AuthorHouse    11/13/2015*

*ISBN: 978-1-5049-5944-5 (sc)*
*ISBN: 978-1-5049-5945-2 (e)*

*Library of Congress Control Number: 2015918196*

*Print information available on the last page.*

*Any people depicted in stock imagery provided by Thinkstock are models, and such images are being used for illustrative purposes only. Certain stock imagery © Thinkstock.*

*This book is printed on acid-free paper.*

# Contents

## Poetic Gifts of Inspiration

# Acknowledgments

Thanks first to God for speaking to my heart and inspiring me to write a message of forgiveness and hope.

A special thanks, too, to my administrator, who encouraged me to write and granted me time away from my work to put my message on paper.

Thank you, Marg Rehnberg, for your willingness to use your creative gifts to design the cover for this book.

And finally, thank you to my dear friends who believed in me and encouraged me along the way to follow the project through to the end.

# Dedication

*Becoming*

This book is dedicated to my dear childhood friend and her husband. My friend struggled many years in her battle with cancer, and her husband lovingly cared for her through the difficult challenges. These friends were the first people to read my manuscript. In the last months of her life, her husband would read to her at night before they turned out the lights. She told me they could hardly put the book down, that it spoke to their hearts. Their encouragement and affirmation of the writing gave me the courage to pursue a publisher.

My last visit with them was the day before she died. I had made the visit to tell her that I was planning to dedicate my book to her and her husband. Although she was heavily medicated and near death, she opened her eyes when I spoke with her. I believe she knew I was there. She entered heaven the next day.

Thank you, beloved friend, for your friendship, your love, and your affirmation. I will look forward to our glorious reunion in paradise.

# Prelude

Have you ever struggled with your own self-esteem?

Did you ever wish you could be like someone else?

Have you ever looked at someone else and said, "Can you believe what they did? I thought they were better than that," or, "What's wrong with them? See, I told you they were messed up."

Have you ever cried yourself to sleep and wished that your life could be different?

Have you ever been in a group of people when they started talking negatively about someone and you chimed into the conversation and talked negatively about another person or group of people? Come on now, tell the truth. I think we have all done that on occasion, but we are not proud of it.

Have you ever cried out and said I am alone or afraid or I am all screwed up?

Good news—there is hope for all of us! This book is for you!

It is my hope that you who have struggled might find peace, hope, purpose, forgiveness, and joy.

For those who have pointed a finger at someone else, I hope that you might experience compassion, forgiveness, renewed purpose, and joy.

Mine is a long journey—a journey of fear, of pain, of rejection, of sin. It's a journey of forgiveness, of perseverance, of more sin, of more forgiveness, of victory, peace, and incredible joy!

Come walk with me now on the journey. Along the way I hope you will see yourself and, just maybe, see someone else whom you either love or dislike. I hope you will be honest with yourself and not be afraid to touch some of those deep, dark secrets you carry at the center of your soul.

I hope as we walk together that you will begin to better understand the love and grace of the creator of the universe, the one who is the maker of all that is good. I hope that by the end of the journey you will know without question that you are fearfully and wonderfully made and that *nothing* can separate you from the one who gave you life. Are you ready? Let's go.

# Just a Little Squirt

"I'm sorry, I'm sorry, I didn't mean to. It was an accident." I was four or five years old at the time. I cried, and I was very afraid. It seemed like it took forever to get home. As a child, when I was upset, I would chew on the bottom of my dress where the sand collected in the hem. It's strange what we do as kids with no clue why! I chewed on my dress all the way home because I knew I was going to get hit when we got home. As I think about it now, it is amazing that I didn't get in trouble for chewing on my dress. You can just imagine what the hem looked like if I was chewing on it all the time. Maybe that was when I started biting my fingernails!

You probably want to know what I did that made me so sorry. I was running through my grandparents' house (really they were my great-grandparents, but I did not know this until my teenage years). I ran through the dining room into the living room and kicked the front door open with my foot to run outside. Instead of kicking the wood frame of the door, I put my foot through the screen. In those days, there were no such things as aluminum or vinyl screen doors. That did it. I knew I was in big trouble—not with my grandpa and grandma. My grandparents were wonderful, gentle people, even if they were from the wrong side of the tracks. I never experienced anything from them but unconditional love, but I was afraid to stay overnight with them. I had been programmed from a very early age to think stereotypically and with prejudice about people based on their occupation or where they lived. It's very subtle, you know.

Anyway, I knew I was going to get it when we got home. Unfortunately, I had already learned to be afraid of my father. I am sure there were other experiences before this that started me on the road to fear, which led to lying. Now when I look back, I know that my behavior was an attempt to protect myself from his anger, to avoid being physically punished. I was punished in other ways as well. His demeaning verbal abuse early on led to my poor self-esteem, but that was much more subtle. The violence that was the result of his anger hurt me physically as well as emotionally, and I tried to protect myself in every way I could.

A cribbage board is a thick board with lots of small holes in it to fit small pegs. I never learned to play or understand the game. All I knew was that it hurt when you got hit with it, and I never wanted to become friends with it. When I was about five or six, I hid it. Silly little kid—how could I not know that he would find it and the punishment would be worse?

One important thing for you to know is that my father loved me. Some said I was his favorite. He showed me lots of affection when I was young (so my relatives say), and I was the apple of his eye. What's wrong with this picture?

Very early in my life, I learned that when people are angry, they hurt you. I learned that I needed to do whatever was necessary to protect myself. I needed to say and do whatever was necessary to please people so that they would not hurt me. It was cause and effect. You misbehave, you get in trouble, and you get hurt. You make a mistake, you have an accident, and you get hurt. Sometimes you get hurt and don't even know why.

I have a few other memories from this early time in my life that would further reinforce my need to protect myself. They will also help you to better understand why I felt so alone and afraid in my most formative years.

We were at my aunt and uncle's house for the weekend, about three hours away from home. This was my mother's brother, the proper, rigid one. This was my first inkling that my father did not like my uncle. I was awakened by my mother in what seemed like the middle of the night. She dressed me and put my shoes on. She said we were going home. I walked into the living room and saw my father on top of my uncle, pinning him to the floor. (My father was big and strong.) I don't remember any words, just the feeling of fear. We went home.

Soon after that experience, my aunt and uncle came to our town. We were on our way to church, walking on the sidewalk, when I saw them coming toward us. I was immediately afraid. What would happen when these adults met? Were they going to fight again? They came closer, and my fear increased. They passed on the sidewalk, and nothing was said. We all went into the church like nothing had happened.

Sometime later, we were planning to go to my mother's parents' cabin for the weekend. The phone call came. My father was mad. My uncle and his family were going to the cabin. Our weekend was spoiled. We could not go. I guess you can tell by now that my father disliked my mother's brother very much. To my knowledge, this relationship was never restored.

How are we doing at building self-esteem in this little squirt? There is a lot more. No wonder it took me so long to get a grip on it. When I turned sixty, my oldest son gave me a mug that said, "Finally, getting a handle on life at sixty!" I said, "Better at sixty than never at all!" Thank God that I have thirty more years to live, celebrate, and be the person who God intended me to be from the beginning. I hope that you do not have to wait so long. But however long it takes you, know that the journey is worth the effort. The peace, safety, and joy that you experience when you reach the mountaintop will be well worth every step along the way.

I was the youngest of three children, a girl with two brothers who are two and five and half years older. My mother always said that I was the apple of my father's eye. She said that she always wanted a girl and that the happiest day of her life was when I was born. Surely I should have felt safe and loved if my father wanted me and I was the answer to my mother's dreams. They were both human, wounded, and fighting for their own lives. How could they possibly show love and protection to their children if they were wounded and suffering themselves?

The foundation for a person's future is laid early in life. If we learn how to respond to life's experiences through our own suffering and lack of nurturing, we become handicapped and unable to respond in a healthy way to pain, sorrow, disappointment, and joy—the realities of life. My hope for you is that if you have been wounded, you will be healed and freed, enabled to experience life as God intended for all humankind.

Below are some phrases I recall that ring perfectly with the reality of my childhood. In hindsight, they help to explain some of my experiences and the decisions I have made along my journey. They help me better understand why I used to have such difficulty expressing feeling or even owning my emotions.

- Brave little girls don't cry.
- If you don't stop crying, I'll give you something to cry about.
- Crying is a sign of weakness.
- Tears are manipulative.
- Children are to be seen and not heard.
- Parents are always right.
- You must always be strong—especially when other people are watching you.
- Anger is bad; never express your anger.
- Good Christians never express negative feelings.

Do any of these phrases ring a bell with you? I now know that any emotion not expressed will be paid for later on with compounded interest. It will not simply go away. What a comfort it was to me when I finally sought some help at the age of forty-three to be told that feelings were neither right nor wrong; they were information. In essence, I was not bad if I had feelings that others might have thought questionable. Did you ever have any feelings that you were afraid to talk about? It's okay; you are normal! What a release. It was okay to say I felt something; feeling that way did not make me a bad person. That was great news, and it was just the beginning of freedom for me.

There are a few violent experiences that have impacted my life in powerful ways; therefore, I write about them. I am sure there were many more experiences that have impacted me that do not remain in the forefront of my thinking. All I know is that fear of violence is something that shaped my life from a very early age, and its effect on me was a factor in my decision-making until I became a senior citizen. Take the dinner table. When I was young, all good families sat down at the table and shared the evening meal together. That was supposed to be what we would call today quality family time.

This was not so in my home. I was continually thinking about what not to say and avoiding certain subjects so that no one would get angry or hurt. It did not take long for me to either be quiet at the table or make jokes. I learned early on to be the life of the party—just pretend that everything is okay. We looked like the ideal family on the block. Even to the day of his death, no one in my parents' circle of close friends had any idea that my father had a violent thread in him. My mother, who was afraid herself, certainly would never have told anyone. After all, what was important was to look good and keep anything that went on in your home to yourself. How dare you ever tell the truth!

There are three significant experiences of physical abuse that are in the forefront of my memory. The pain and the sadness are as raw as if they occurred yesterday, and they happened more than fifty years ago.

This is what I mean about the impact of painful experiences in our lives. Do you have any such experiences that are as fresh now as they were fifty years ago? Believe me, the pain never goes away, but our ability to cope with the pain and understand it is the key to being free and being bound by it no longer.

Even in recent years I have awakened from a bad dream where I'm eight years old and watching the blood swirl down the drain in the bathroom sink. I lean my head over the sink to catch the blood coming from my nose. Again, my father had lost control, and this time he had hit me in the head. I stood alone in the bathroom wearing the hideous purple and chartreuse sundress that my mother had so lovingly created, trying not to get the blood on my dress so that I would not get in trouble again. I didn't want to have to make up another story about where the blood came from because I could not tell the truth. Of course, as had been the case in most of the violence I had experienced so far, my mother was at work. My father was at home because he worked a variety of shifts, switching every seven weeks. This helped to take care of the need to pay for childcare, as money was always tight in our family. (That is a whole different story that has also impacted me to this day—money, how we live, how we spend it, and our attitude toward it.)

You want to know what I did this time to draw his anger? It was bad—really bad! Believe me, as a parent I too would have been beside myself. And if it weren't for the powerful work of God in my own life, I likely would have done something similar. I don't think I would have hit my child in the face, but what difference does that make? To strike a child out of one's anger is wrong, and it is incredibly destructive.

My father had just finished building our new house (while still working at his full-time job). I was painting my toenails on the floor at the foot of my parents' bed on the new carpet without so much as a washcloth, paper towel, or anything to protect the carpet. Red fingernail polish, mind you, on light-green carpet. I knocked the bottle over and speckled the carpet with a few colorful spots of red. If that wouldn't make a parent upset, I don't know what would. It was brand-new carpet in a brand-new house, and there certainly was no money to replace the carpet. Besides that, the damaged carpet was likely installed on borrowed money that would not be paid back for a very long time. You bet he was mad, and I was way out of line.

The sad thing is that because he did not know how to control his anger, the impact of his rage affected my life in terrible ways forever after. I do not remember anything about what happened after my nose stopped bleeding other than that he was on his hands and knees scrubbing the floor. I went into my room and shut the door. I never told a soul about what happened.

The next time my father was feeling good and put his arm around me, I was supposed to forget what happened. I guess he was able to get the spots out of the carpet because I never heard it mentioned again. Basically, I just shoved every feeling down inside of myself, increasingly felt worse and worse about who I was, continued to lie, and became more and more afraid.

The little squirt grew into a tomboy with a whole lot of baggage that would be sure to surface over and over again in the years to come.

# Images and Wounded Gifts

When I am surrounded by nature in peaceful places, I am always reminded of the awesome wonder of God's creation. So many images come to mind. God often speaks to me there. When I am away from the stress of everyday life, when I take the time to be quiet, the voice of God becomes loud and clear. I am so grateful for God's voice. I now know that there is nowhere I can go, nothing that I can think, and nothing that I can do that will separate me from God's incredible love. I did not always know this truth.

As I write this chapter, I am sitting on the grass in the sun, overlooking the Pacific Ocean and the mountains that surround the bay in Puerto Vallarta, Mexico. I often see much imagery in nature that is synonymous with life.

Let's talk about stones for a minute. If you asked ten people to describe a stone or a rock, do you think you would get the same answer from each person? No, probably not. For some, a rock is a hard, jagged thing. It can hurt you if you step on it. It can hurt others if they are hit by it. It may not be anything beautiful but rather something that causes pain. Life is full of rocks—hard, jagged rocks.

For others, stones are beautiful, often interesting and smooth, wonderful reminders of creation. Think about precious stones, like the beauty and value of diamonds. How many times have you heard someone say, "They are a diamond in the rough"? When diamonds come out of the earth, they are rough and unpolished. But as they are polished, they become beautiful. So it is with people. God knows the beauty that is inside once we are stripped of our rough exterior. Deep in the center of our being, every person is beautiful, uniquely designed, and crafted by the creator of life. We are each extremely valuable.

Somehow though, as we experience the difficult times in our lives, many become hardened and develop rough exteriors to protect themselves from pain and suffering. If the tender, beautiful interior is not exposed, it cannot be damaged or hurt. Life often teaches us not to feel in order to protect ourselves. We develop defense mechanisms for self-protection, not because we are bad or malicious people, but rather because we are precious, wounded persons trying to survive.

I was walking on the beach in the early morning. Small stones brought in by the tide were lined up along the beach all in a row. Picture it for a moment. The tide brought them in all in a line, thicker in some places than others, but all in a line, only going so far onto the beach and then stopping. Amazing! Some were smooth and some were rough. My first thought was that they should all be smooth. Why not? They had all been washed onto the beach by the sea. I expected them all to be perfect, but they were not. Maybe some had been in the water longer, washed again and again by the sea and made smooth. Maybe the rough ones were recently thrown into the sea; maybe they had never before been washed by the purifying, cleansing, sometimes abrasive flow of the tide. How long does it take for them to become smooth? I am guessing that depends on how rough they were when they went into the water.

It is the same with people. Some have never been very rough. Others have been wounded over and over again and have protected themselves with a hard, rough outer shell. On the inside they are still beautiful, magnificent creatures, but unfortunately they either go through life unnoticed or, even worse, rejected by others. Consequently, they cannot see themselves as beautiful and have difficulty comprehending the meaning of unconditional love. Do you know anyone like that? Are you like that? Or are you one of those stones that never was very rough when it went into the sea? Sometimes it is hard to comprehend what we have not experienced.

Psalm 139 says that we are all fearfully and wonderfully made; that we are the marvelous workmanship of the creator. Today I believe from the bottom of my heart that all persons are born with value and worth, each one uniquely gifted and created. I also believe that we all came into the world as innocent, precious masterpieces, but that from the time of our birth we have been molded and shaped by the circumstances of our lives and by relationships that have either affirmed us or hurt us. Human beings are vulnerable and often fall prey to the cruel injustices of a broken and sinful world. Too often, God's precious gifts become wounded (some more so than others), and life becomes a matter of survival. Rather than being an opportunity to experience the wonder of God's creation to the fullest, life becomes a matter of endurance, of suffering, of coping, of finding ways to get by with the least amount of pain. Oftentimes the way we choose to cope when we are vulnerable is not only destructive to ourselves but to others as well. It has been said that "hurting people hurt people."

My father was a gift, but wounded and out of control. I am grateful that I can call him a gift today. This was not always so. My father was a very talented man. He was the one from whom I received my creative inspiration to design and write. All of my artistic ability was inspired by him. I can remember sitting with him at the kitchen table as a young child while he showed me how to draw people. The sad part was that if I did not do it to his satisfaction, I was scolded. I soon learned that nothing I did was good enough for him. The formation of my self-esteem was eroding before it even had a chance to develop.

I specifically remember one Christmas when I was in the late elementary grades. I received a paint-by-numbers gift, and I was really excited about it. In the afternoon on Christmas day, I was in my room painting on my new gift. The next thing I knew, my father was looking at it, telling me what I did wrong, asking me why I didn't ask for help before I screwed it up. I was devastated by his comments. He was a perfectionist and expected that same kind of perfection from me. All I remember is that I did it wrong, he was not pleased with me, and the joy of my Christmas was ruined. Did my father deliberately try to hurt me? No, of course not. He simply was responding to me in the only way he knew how. It's easy to ask why he didn't know how destructive his rejection was to my self-esteem.

I know very little about my father's family, but I do know his mother was married several times. I don't believe she was ever married to his father, about whom he knew very little. He knew nothing of the special relationship that God intended for fathers and their children. I doubt that he ever knew the safety and affirmation of a loving, understanding parent. Please don't misunderstand. His grandparents were loving people who would reach out to anyone and everyone. I know that when he was born, he was brought to their home, and they cared for him as if he was their own. His mother did not live with him, nor did she play any positive or significant role in his life. Her name was Lenore. Every few years at Christmastime, Lenore would come to our house bearing gifts. My brothers and I thought it was great. Though he never said anything, it was clear that he did not like her and definitely was not excited about her visits. He never referred to her as his mother. I am sure he lived his whole life longing for the love of "real" parents, a mother and a father who would protect him, love him, encourage his dreams and say, "Well done." Was that really too much for a child to ask? Of course it was not. It is not only the wish of every child but of every adult as well. We all want to be loved, affirmed, and encouraged for who we are just because we are.

I had the feeling that even though he called his grandparents Mom and Pop, they were older, and he was treated more like someone else's child rather than as their own. Lenore had a brother who showed love to him and our family, and occasionally we would visit this uncle's family.

But there was always some underlying sense that these people were not as valuable as they were on my mother's side of the family. I am sure my maternal grandparents thought everything about my father came from "the wrong side of the tracks." After all, he didn't have a father, didn't even know who his father was, and his mother had abandoned him. What kind of a public image was that? Public image was extremely important to my mother's parents. My parents grew up during the Depression, when most of America suffered economically. Because my mother's father worked for the city, their family was not as significantly impacted by the Depression. I think my grandfather thought he was better than other folks. My father's "father" (really his grandfather) was a longshoreman who worked down on the docks. You know, one of the rougher, more unpolished types. And they didn't go to church.

It seemed to me that people liked my father. He cared about people who were hurting. He valued people for who they were based on his relationship with them. He often invited people to the house, even people who were different from our typical middle-class family. I specifically remember a man who shared a hospital room with my father when I was about ten. The man was Hispanic. (That was a big deal to some people. There definitely were no Hispanic families in our new, up-and-coming neighborhood, only white, middle-class families.) The man's leg had been amputated as a result of a fall from scaffolding on his job. He had a young family. My father invited the family to our house, and they came when the young man received his prostheses. It was a joyful meeting, a time of celebration. My father didn't go to church very often, but I think he showed love to hurting people.

Life was hard for my father. He had big dreams. He was bright and talented. He wanted to go to a private university, but there was no money to finance his dream. He had a variety of jobs in his short life. In the early years of my parents' marriage, I think he pursued his dreams only to have something go wrong time and time again. I know finances were always an issue, and it seemed our family never had enough. I am guessing that this probably contributed much to his feelings of failure and defeat. My mother worked from before the time I went to school, which was pretty unusual back then. My father worked many years as a truck driver in the oil fields but was embarrassed to tell anyone what he did. He always dreamed of a better day. That day never came. Along with his full-time job, he built a total of seven homes for our family and was just completing a thirteen-unit apartment building before his untimely death at the age of forty-two.

Emotionally, I think my father was a mess. Of course, no one talked about emotional health in those days unless it was in reference to someone who was mentally ill, and heaven forbid if you had "one of those" in your family. The expectations he placed on himself were great because he was a perfectionist. The expectations my mother placed on him were probably great too. The expectations of his in-laws were always there. I am guessing he felt frustrated most of the time. I think he might have often felt like he could not win because he would say, "I can't win for losing." How did he deal with all of the pressure? How did he deal with the basic unmet human needs in his life? He erupted in anger and became out of control when things did not go as he thought they should or when he felt rejected. He was not a bad person, just very wounded and without power beyond himself to overcome his anger.

I can honestly say that my mother too was a gift. For much of my life it was difficult for me to recognize her giftedness. I thank God today that I can affirm her with my whole heart. I wish I had been more able to express my appreciation for her while she was alive, but I believe God understands that, and I do think she knew that I loved her by the way I responded to her in the last twelve years of her life.

My mother was seventy-five years old when she finally said out loud for the first time in her life that my father hit her. My brother had told me this was so, but I had never actually seen my father hit her. They fought often. I think I was too busy just trying to protect myself from eruption of his anger that I was not aware of building tensions between them. I do remember pleading with him when I was about twelve not

13

to leave our family. There was an incredible stigma attached to single-parent families in those days. I certainly did not want to become one of those statistics, even if the family was unbelievably dysfunctional.

My mother too was a perfectionist. She was an excellent seamstress, an immaculate housekeeper, and a wonderful cook. She prided herself in making everything from scratch. She often judged others by whether their food was homemade or store-bought. The clothes my mother made me were far superior to any dress you could buy at J. C. Penney, and she made me a new dress for every special occasion in which I was ever involved. She often stayed up most of the night to make me something new for some special event. She was a wife, a homemaker, a mother of three, a seamstress, and employed full-time, mostly in doctors' offices in my early and elementary years. I get tired just thinking about it!

I always wished that I could just once have a store-bought dress. I specifically remember one year before school started that my father took me shopping and bought me three new dresses. They were plaid. I clearly remember chewing the hem on those dresses. I remember my father saying that he was getting them for me because my mother did not have time to make what I needed for school. But rather than pleasing my mother, I think she was irritated or angry that he had bought them. Maybe it was about spending the money. Maybe it was about the quality. But I do know she was not happy about it. Likely, it was another one of those times when my father felt he "could not win for losing."

My mother did not know how to show affection. It was not that she did not feel emotion; she simply did not know how to express her feelings. I think this was fairly common for her generation. As recently as just a few years ago, I talked with childhood friends who said the same things about their mothers. One even went so far as to say that her mother told her that if she told her daughter she did something well, she would get a "big head." How sad! This, of course, was all before the printing of the book *I'm OK, You're OK*.

Neither my brothers nor I have any memory of our mother holding us, putting her arms around us, or telling us that we were loved. (My grown daughter commented that my mother meant well, but that she just was not comforting—such a profound observation.) The only thing I can remember my mother saying consistently when I was young was "Good night, sleep tight, don't let the bed bugs bite." Where is the comfort in that for a little kid? I bet you might remember that too.

After my father's death, I learned a lot about my mother. Her life was hard. Her life with my father was always based on a dream that never materialized. I only lived in one of those seven houses my father built. The others were all built before I was born. My mother lived in all of them for a short time. Though I never heard her complain about it, I am sure life for her during the construction of each house was a chapter in itself. She mostly talked about the big house on Red Road. That was before I was born, when she was twenty-eight. What she talked less about was the trailer they lived in with no running water. She did talk some about the garage they lived in with no running water and no bathroom, with a two-and-a-half-year-old and a newborn. Remember, status was very important to my mother's family. Do you think this life was my grandparents' wish for their daughter? Would it be your wish for yours? I seriously doubt it.

Everyone has dreams when they get married. I doubt this was my mother's dream, yet she spoke of this time in her life without any inference of pain or disappointment. She talked about washing the diapers outside, about my father falling in the hole dug for the well, and about the lambs, Mary and Mary Ann, eating the bark off of the avocado trees and dying. She talked about the huge St. Bernard dog named Queenie and how much she ate. Even though she never appreciated our other dog, Skeeter, she always talked warmly about Queenie. She talked warmly about their friends in the small community in which they lived, friends who remained in contact with her almost up until the time of her death in 2006.

My mother was a pretender. If you could paint a happy picture, then life was happy. If you simply did not talk about the troubles, you could hope they would go away or you could deny they existed. It made life easier. We all have done that. But the reality is, if we do not deal with life realistically, it does not go away, and steps cannot be taken to improve our lives. It took me a very long time to be honest with my inner thoughts. It took even longer for me acknowledge them, deal with them, and experience the freedom of a lighter load.

Each of my brothers is gifted in different ways. Each has been wounded in ways that have profoundly affected their lives. Each has experienced at least one failed marriage, and we have all taken wrong turns upon more than one occasion.

From my earliest memory, it seemed as if my oldest brother was continually in trouble. It seemed like he was always testing the waters, but that may not have been the case at all. He was five and a half years older than I was. When I was about three, my mother gave him money to get his hair cut. He came home with the center of his head shaved—like a very, very short flattop. I can see the picture now. I think he was very proud of his haircut. I don't think it set well with my parents, at least not my mother, but I will never know. I can remember the three of us in twin beds lined up a row in the bedroom, all being punished for lighting a fire in the vacant lot down the street beyond the trailer park. However, in all fairness to my oldest brother, I think the marshmallow roast was my other brother's idea. My job was to climb up on the counter and get the marshmallows and bring them and the matches to the vacant lot. I think the fence caught on fire.

When I was in preschool, to my mother's horror, my oldest brother brought home a snake. He kept it in a large box in the garage and fed it egg yolks. Then there was the pet mouse or white rat that got loose in the house, and my mother found it in the drawers in the built-in buffet in the dining area. My mother was pretty naive and always dramatic. Next, he brought home his best friend Skeeter, the mutt my mother hated and used to kick off the back porch. Little did she know that Skeeter, on every possible occasion, would get in the back door and race through the house from one end to the other, as if the house was on fire. My memory of this brother was that he was always on the edge, a little daring, mischievous, and secretive.

It seemed that life for him grew worse with each new day. Today he says that he can remember hating our father from the time he was four years old. Although this brother was bright, he did poorly in school. He stuttered, and this made life even more difficult for him. He first ran away from home when I was nine years old. I will always remember the empty feeling, the fear and the sadness. I think my great-grandparents went to get him and Skeeter in the freight train yard in the nearby big city. He ran away again when I was ten and he was fifteen. This time he was gone for what seemed like forever. He was about to cross the state line about a thousand miles from home when he was picked up by the police. He was small for his age. In that day it was not unusual for people to hitchhike, but he looked like he was too young. (I think he had been gone for about four days.) He was put in jail until my father could go and get him. Imagine the royal reception he received when my father arrived at the jail and they met face to face. Definitely not a warm reunion!

I often hurt for this brother. He always treated me with kindness, but he was in trouble so often I think I was afraid to identify too closely with him. I think I thought that if I stayed out of trouble, life would be better for me. I tried never to break the rules. Maybe a better way to say it is that I worked very hard at never getting caught doing anything wrong.

I wouldn't say that my two brothers fought a lot. I really cannot remember, but it seemed like they did not like each other very much. They were very different from one another. They had very different circles of friends, and their interests were as different as night and day.

When these boys were growing up, black leather jackets and motorcycles were reserved for Hells Angels. It was assumed that those who wore them sold and used heroin in the back alleys and dark streets of big cities. We lived in the big city. My oldest brother wore a black leather jacket and rode a motorcycle. What was I to think? I don't know about the drugs, but I know that he consumed more than his share of alcohol.

This brother was very mechanically inclined. I remember he could fix just about anything. I don't remember that he was ever interested in sports. My first memories of his troubles in school were in junior high school, and it seemed like they compounded with every year through high school. One day after school when I was in sixth grade, he took me for a ride and told me that he had not been to school for eighteen days. I was shocked. I was a good student. That was unthinkable! I wasn't supposed to tell anyone, and I didn't tell anyone—until now. He was kicked out of school. He finally finished at a continuation high school where every other girl in the graduating class was pregnant, which was most unusual and very scandalous fifty years ago.

By now that image of status and what people thought was pretty well ingrained in me. Is it any wonder that this brother preferred my father's grandparents to my mother's parents? For me, his graduation ceremony was a mixture of happy and sad emotions. I was glad that my brother had finally graduated from high school but saddened that he could not finish at a "regular" public school like everyone else I knew. He joined the service at the age of seventeen with his father's signature and was finally free from the tyranny of his father's wrath. He never returned to live in our home community but rather settled in Alaska far away from his roots.

My second brother was our father's delight. He was a natural-born athlete, just what any father would wish for. He was a good student, never got in trouble, was "Mr. Popular," and had a large circle of respectable friends. In some ways, I think my father lived his dreams through this brother's accomplishments. Life seemed easy for this brother. My parents and I went to his baseball and basketball games, and our father went to his track meets when he could. He looked forward to a full-ride college scholarship and a bright future. He had a great sense of humor and could make us laugh. He collected practical joke gadgets, especially the ones you could use at the table, like the fly on a pin that could be stuck in the butter or the etched glass that would drip when you tilted it to take a drink. And then there was that gadget that went under the toilet seat that would squirt water when you sat down. You get the idea. He was a jokester, but he did not talk about feelings. Unlike my oldest brother, he would reveal very little about what he was thinking or feeling. However, it was clear when he was angry.

Ironically, I was closest to this brother, even though our oldest brother was the one who treated me with tenderness and kindness. I know this did not make sense to my oldest brother. I have fond memories of my second brother and me riding the bike to the golf course several miles from our home. He rode on the seat and I on the handle bars with golf clubs in tow.

He was three years ahead of me in school, so we never attended the same school in our junior high or high school years. He was an all-around athlete and excelled in football, basketball, and track. In his senior year in high school, I believe he set a track record in the state and participated in a three-state invitational. He received a track scholarship to a university in the northern part of our state.

When he reached his late teens, he scared me when he was mad. I have memories of him chasing me through the house with a butcher knife. On another occasion when I did something that angered him, he grabbed me by the arm and threw me from the hallway out into the living room. My closer relationship with this brother did not make sense to my oldest brother and was hurtful to him. Although they showed it in different ways, both of my brothers had that same potential to be out

19

of control when their buttons were pushed. Our role model for dealing with anger was not the best.

Unlike my oldest brother, this brother did not talk to me about what he was thinking or feeling. I am not sure he ever talked to anyone about his feelings. Expressing emotion seemed pretty foreign to him, but I know that there was plenty of feeling buried somewhere deep inside of him.

After high school graduation he went away to college on a track scholarship, but he only stayed in school for one semester. He dropped out and moved to Alaska, where my oldest brother was living. I will never forget the shock when he sent a newspaper clipping to my mother telling about his being jailed for an altercation with another young man. Apparently he and his friend were at a party, and someone began pistol-whipping his friend. I don't know how long he was in jail, but I do remember my oldest brother talking about the incident and saying that my brother just about maimed the other person for life. Can you imagine my mother's reaction when she received this clipping in the mail? Just what my mother wanted to hear, that her "perfect" son had been arrested and jailed for his out of control behavior. I have often wondered why he sent the clipping to her.

After a year in Alaska and some world travel, this second brother came back home and re-enrolled in college. He spent time in the service then completed his college education and became a teacher. He got married and settled down with his family in a place far away from the land of his youth. Like our father, he experienced some very serious health problems at a very early age, some as a result of exposure to Agent Orange in Vietnam. He has been totally disabled for many years now. I hear from him several times a year, and occasionally he hears from our oldest brother. It was only recently that he told me that he remembers very little about his childhood other than the beatings. I was shocked to hear that he too had been abused by our father.

We have all been wounded in one way or another. I wish it were not so. However, I decided a long time ago that life for my children did not have to be like my own family experience. I wanted so much to have the opportunity to offer a different picture of home and family, a safer picture. Although it was not the perfect family experience (if there is such a thing), I think our children can say that their parents did not repeat the same mistakes of their grandparents. We tried to always affirm our children and support them in all that they did. We tried not to be judgmental and assured them of our love for them. We tried to teach them that people were more important than things and that if they expected to be forgiven, they needed to forgive. We tried to teach them that the way Jesus lived his life on this earth was our example. It is with great joy that we now watch each of our children as parents teaching these same values to their own children. We can never change what has been, but we can always strive to make a difference in the future. We can hold onto the hope that, although we are wounded and scarred, God is not finished with us yet!

Maybe we are all wounded gifts. I believe every human being has areas of strength and areas of weakness. I am so thankful that God loves us in spite of our weaknesses, encourages us to grow and become, and calls us to look for the good in others. May we continually strive to show love to all in this troubled world.

# Hormones, Rough Roads, and Confusion

Hold onto your hat. This is where life gets very interesting and all mixed up.

Adolescence was quite a trip for me. As I tell this story, some of the experiences may seem familiar to you. Hopefully, your journey was not as traumatic as mine, but I know that for most people, growing into adulthood produced some mighty hurdles along the way.

When I think of adolescence, I think of changing hormones and changing bodies. I think of boys and girls expanding their worlds to include heterosexual relationships. I think of giggling girls and makeup and the need to be noticed. I think of boys needing to look just right, needing to be cool. I think of peer pressure and the need to be included. I think of the need to be understood by parents and the need to have someone in whom you can confide. I think of first kisses, first dances, phone conversations, and exploring new and often forbidden territory.

Adolescence for me was a time of conflicting emotions. It was a time of developing sexuality, of poor self-esteem, of violence and death. It was a painful time and lonely time, a time when I often felt misunderstood. It was a time when I felt incredibly insecure. Adolescence was a time I would like to forget, but it's also a memory that will never go completely away. However, I do know that the person I am today is the direct result of that awful time in my younger years, the wrong choices in my life, and my deep desire to be free and whole. Would I have wished for the painful experiences of my past? No, never! But I had the choice to be either bound by my pain and thus compromise the life that God intended for me or go for it, face the pain, learn about myself, and trust God to take care of me. I have chosen to say yes to the journey that has brought me to this place of peace and security today. To start on the journey earlier in life would have been good, but it is better to be late to the starting line than to never begin the journey at all. Where are you on your own journey to peace and security?

I was a tomboy, a natural-born athlete. In the late elementary grades, I received affirmation for my athletic ability. I was also a good student. I was an overachiever, so I was always out to get the extra-credit points. I needed to receive affirmation wherever I could because I seldom experienced it at home. My parents (my father especially) had high expectations for me. Unfortunately, it felt like I could never do anything well enough, no matter how hard I tried. Do you know that experience? Doesn't make you feel very secure, does it?

My father was very controlling, and I learned early on that when he told me to do something, I should do it. As I came into the teenage years, I began to resist his control. There was no reasoning with my father; at least, that is how it seemed then. As I look back now, I really don't know whether he was that unreasonable or not. I just know that I was afraid to express my feelings, and I was afraid of him.

I remember telling my mother that I was afraid of him, but she provided little or no comfort. I could never understand why she did not come to my defense. It was not until she was seventy-five years old that I learned that she too was afraid of him. She was simply unable to stand up for me because of her own fear. Her lack of protection or intervention on my behalf had nothing to do with her feelings for me, but it took me a very long time to recognize and understand this.

I remember the first time I experimented with eye makeup. When my father saw me, he insisted that I go into the bathroom and take that "crap" off of my eyes. It wasn't like I had overdone it or that I looked like a clown; he simply did not like makeup and wasn't going to have his daughter wearing it. What other choice did I have but to hide my experimentation from him and slide into a world of secrecy and lies?

Music and the teenage years go together, right? Not so at our house. My father had the radio set to his music (which, of course, the kids did not appreciate), and he would not tolerate it if we changed the station. Of course we changed the station when he was not there, but from time to time we forgot to change it back. We would always hear about it. For me, it became easier to withdraw into myself, stay away from his wrath, and somehow try to find affirmation and acceptance any way I could.

Since I could not find it at home, I tried to find it at school. The junior high years were basically good years for me. I was fortunate to have good friends in the early adolescent years, and I received positive affirmation at school as a good student and as an athlete. I never talked about what it was like at home, and I seldom brought friends to the house.

I said I was a tomboy. My body began to change rapidly as an adolescent. I was tall and shapely, but still a tomboy at heart. My understanding of puberty, sexuality, and reproduction was way behind my physical development. I think boys were attracted to my body, but emotionally I was a late bloomer and very naive, so much of the time I just didn't get it. My days as a "tease" probably began way back then, when I wasn't even aware of it.

Our school had what they called the "Canteen," a place where kids gathered on Thursday and Friday nights to dance and hang out. I wanted to go on a Thursday night (because that was the in thing to do). I asked my mother if I could go. Of course, she needed to ask my father, and he said no. I pleaded with him to let me go, and he was adamant that I could not go. (When I think about it now, I likely would not have given my own daughter permission to go to a dance on a school night, even though it was only until 9:00 p.m.).

I was pretty strong willed even as a teenager. My father and I argued, and the next thing I knew, I was telling my father that I hated him. And that was it. He started to hit me. I ran to my bedroom, and he came after me. I lay down on the bed, and he sat of top of me and hit my head and face back and forth. My mother was in the kitchen, clearly hearing what was going on, and she never intervened. When I was able to get away from him, I ran into the bathroom and locked the door. My father was a big man, and I thought he was going to break the door down. I was hurt, both physically and emotionally, and very much afraid. I stayed in the bathroom for a while, and when I came out, I could hear my father crying in his bedroom.

I am sure now that telling my father I hated him was just too much for him to bear and his only response was to lash out in anger. I know I hurt him deeply, and I was never able to tell him I was sorry. Oh, for the wisdom of old age and experiences past.

Again, my mother was there but did not come to my rescue. I could not understand why. I had seen her stand by and do nothing as he unmercifully hit my older brother when he was sixteen years old, and now she did nothing to protect me. Indeed, I felt very much alone.

I think it was then that I started to cry out to God for protection. I had to go to school the next day with a huge hematoma under my upper lip. When kids asked what happened to me, I told them my father hit me. There was no one else I could tell. I never thought to get help from someone at the school. That would have made my family look bad, and that was an absolute no-no. I simply stuffed all of the emotion and pain down deep inside and pretended it was not there.

My father never apologized to me, nor was there any conversation about the incident. As I stuffed the pain down inside, my low self-esteem and my fear were reinforced. From then on, I avoided confrontation at all cost, stayed away from home as much as possible when my father was home, and continued to find ways to validate my value as a person outside of my family.

By that time, my oldest brother had joined the service at the age of seventeen with parental consent, his way of getting away from our father. My other brother was now in high school, a good student, an athlete, and doing well with a solid group of friends. Interestingly enough, our father thrived on the athletic success of my middle brother, and at that point in time, I thought he was the one who experienced the most favor from our father. It has only been in recent years that I have become aware that he too resented our father. He never told me this, but a friend of his did. I never knew my second brother was beaten too. I understand now that our father would go to his practices, yell from the bleachers at my brother, and embarrass him. Always that perfectionist thing! Just recently on a visit to see this brother, I talked briefly with him about our father. He told me that he remembered very little about his childhood but the thing that he remembered most was the beatings. I was shocked! The sad truth is that we all were injured in one way or another by our father's uncontrolled anger.

Then it happened—that terrible, unforgettable day when I was fourteen. I came home from school alone to find my father, who had been working in the back bathroom, his silent body in a contorted position on the bathroom floor. Fluid had drained out of his mouth into a puddle on the floor, and his right arm was black. I pulled his body out of the bathroom into the laundry room, put a wet cloth on his head, and called 911. I then ran five houses down the street to a friend's house for help. We waited for the ambulance. I was standing on the sidewalk while the paramedics were inside when two of my peers on the student council came walking past the house. I remember saying to them, "I just hope he isn't dead." Of course he was dead, but I had never seen a dead person before, much less touched one!

This was on a Thursday. Ironically, one of the friends who was walking past the house that day experienced the suicide of his own father on the following Sunday. Here we were, two kids on the student council whose fathers had been found dead within four days of each other. Needless to say, we had a friendship based on our experience with death that our peers did not understand. Suicide was ugly, as was abuse and the death of the abuser. At a reunion twenty-five years later, my friend told me it had taken him those intervening decades to understand and accept his father's death, and that had only been possible because of the loving, supportive encouragement of his wife, who was a psychotherapist.

No one ever asked me how I felt about my father's death, and I found no one to confide in about the abuse, the feelings of guilt, and all of the emotion that was piled up inside of me. I felt so alone, I longed to be loved, and I had such low self-esteem that all I could do was put myself down. I could not say anything positive about myself. I could not talk to my mother, who cried all the time and was terrified of being alone. She was overwhelmed financially, and life was very difficult for her. When I needed comfort and understanding, she simply was incapable of helping me. Actually, I think she depended on me emotionally to look after her. She did not even want me to leave her alone on the weekends to go out with friends. I don't believe she ever asked me how I was feeling.

I remember the neighbor to whom I had gone for help encouraging me to cry, but I could not. I had just found the man who abused me dead. I was glad he could not hurt me anymore. I felt guilty for not feeling sad. I was numb and alone. The only time I cried was when I saw him at the mortuary in what they called the "slumber room." It was far more grotesque than finding him dead. For at least twenty years after his funeral, I did not go to a viewing because of the terrible memory of my father in that casket. The memory was of makeup and face powder and people saying, "Didn't they do a nice job?" I cried hard then, not because he was dead, but because I wanted to remember what he looked like when I found him, not what he looked like all made up. Remember, I told you he disliked makeup. I am sure he would not have liked the way he looked, either!

There is no question that this abuse and death experience with my father was a turning point in my life. I really think it was then that I started on the downward journey of survival and self-protection, the journey that led me to self-abuse, insecurity, unhappiness, and poor choices.

The high school years were painful for me. My mother and I argued much of the time. She was beside herself with me. In the heat of an argument one time, I remember her saying something to me like, "In the Bible it says …" That really set me off. I said something like, "I don't care what the Bible says." I think what I was reacting to was the fact that my mother was very churchy. To me it meant that she was proper and moral, talked about right and wrong a lot, and went to a church regularly (even if she was always what seemed like half an hour late). But she showed no joy or power for living in her life. She complained a lot. I remember my father saying to my brothers and me, "Do what you are supposed to do so that I don't have to hear about it when I get home."

My mother worked hard. She was gone every day when most other kids' moms were at home, especially when they got home from school. She had bills to pay and was stretched to her limit. She was beautiful and alone with two kids left at home, neither of whom confided in her or experienced love and compassion from her. In those days it was very difficult for me to appreciate the fact that she was a Christian because there was no joy, no power. Life was not good, and it was questionable that anyone in this dysfunctional family was happy.

The downward spiral in my life was well in place by the summer after my ninth grade year. I remember a guy friend, who is still a friend after all these many years, saying to me, "I know your father died, and I am sorry for you, but you cannot keep putting yourself down all the time." Oh, the wisdom of a fifteen-year-old young man! I should have listened then.

I would lie in my bed at night, once the nightmares of my father's return finally stopped, thinking that if only someone would love me, I could do anything, be anything they wanted me to be. I could trade compliance for love and attention. I was well on my way to compromise by this time in my life. If survival involved compromise, it had to be okay. In the years ahead, I would compromise way too many times.

At school most of my peers had no idea what was inside of me. By the high school years, I had learned well how to pretend and to deny feelings. I continued to be an over-achiever and a people pleaser, but by then something had changed. Because of my deep feelings of being rejected, I stopped taking risks. I had been bold enough to run for student council office in junior high and was recognized as a leader. However, my father's death changed everything. I was too afraid of failure in high school, and I was very fearful of anything competitive. I only set out to achieve that which I knew was absolutely possible and nothing more. When I think about it now, it is sad because those high school years could have been great years for me, like they appeared to be for my brother.

I did some things well. I tried out for the drill team, which was for juniors and seniors only, as a junior. That was a cool thing to do. There were a hundred students on the team, and I was elected by my peers to be the captain in my senior year. I was invited by upper-class girls to join the service club for good students and service-minded girls. I tried out for a capella choir and made it. My friends were the popular kids and leaders in student government. I received a scholarship to the local state college, which was considered better than the tuition-free city college, though it really wasn't. So my credentials in the yearbook were above average on paper, but that was as far as it went. What you see is not always what is.

Then there were the boys. By then I was a very well developed young lady who could easily attract the attention of young men growing into manhood. I was soft-spoken, and it was easy for me to talk with guys. Actually, it seemed easier for me to talk with guys than with girls. I was still very naive about male sexual development, and I am sure I frustrated more than one young man. I am grateful that I had very strong convictions about sexual promiscuity because my life could have been forever complicated by wrong choices when it came to sexual exploration. But I was a major tease. I was playful, probably seductive, and then I would run the other way if a guy tried to touch me. I was naive enough to think that that was the way all high school girls were. Little did I know that many of my peers were sexually active by the middle of their teenage years.

I lived in a huge city with five major high schools, and some of the girls' service clubs from one school would have joint meetings with guys' clubs from other schools. Following one such meeting, a very handsome guy called me, and we talked on the phone every day for a couple of weeks. We talked about loving the beach and loving to listen to the waves at night. (To this day I love the sound of the waves breaking on the beach. In fact, as I write this chapter, I am sitting at a table on the beach in Puerto Vallarta, Mexico, listening to the waves break and enjoying the wonder of the breeze. I enjoy the beauty of the landscaping and palm trees and am so keenly aware of the wonder of creation and God's handiwork.) Believe me, when this young man and I were talking on the phone the many times before our big date, the wonder of creation and God's handiwork were not in the forefront of this young man's mind. When we finally got to the beach that memorable night, he laid out the blanket immediately and began to hold me and kiss me. When I resisted his advances, we had a conversation. He said, "I am sorry, I thought you were different. This is not good. I am going to take you home." I think I was home from the date by 9:00 p.m. In the months ahead and in the next few years, I was often misunderstood.

In March of my sophomore year, I began my relationship with my first long-term boyfriend. He was not happy at home and a poor communicator. He was smart but an underachiever who found solace in drinking beer and smoking cigarettes with his other unhappy friends. His father was well educated and rigid, and he ruled the roost. My boyfriend worked hard at not ruffling his father's feathers, but he was secretive and defiant of his father's values and his rules. It is probably not hard to understand that this first love was uncommunicative and could not express emotion. Fortunately for me, he was not sexually aggressive with me and would do just about anything to avoid the wrath of his father, so he did not want to do anything that was questionable.

For the first few months he treated me nicely. Our regular dates were to motorcycle and drag races. I hated both, but a date was better than no date. At least, that is what I thought then. I remember when he was fifteen, he told me he loved me for the first time. I told him to talk to me again when he was sober! Talk about compromise! The relationship continued through the summer, and then when school began in the fall, I still wanted his attention. Some attention was better than none, right? Wrong! He began to test the waters with some of my friends. He would be nasty to me, and then would come back and be nice, and then be nasty again. This continued through the end of our junior year. I had lots of dates during that ugly time, but no one stayed around long. I am not sure why, but I am guessing I pushed them away.

Then it seemed he came back to stay. Why, I do not know. He was my boyfriend through our senior year in high school, and by then most people knew us as a couple. Maybe the fact that we were both emotionally underdeveloped and fearful kept us from being promiscuous. By this time his family had become family to me. They welcomed me and included me in their family experiences. They helped me have spending money by allowing me to clean their house. They were very particular, and I always feared I would not do a good enough job. I even went to church with them. His parents were educated and churchy too. They took me in and showed me love. Sounds like a pretty respectable middle-class family, doesn't it? Believe me, it was not. Jack, the father, had some deviant sexual behavior, some directed toward me, and Marg, the mom, told me she considered me more like a sister. She said that she preferred the company of men rather than women. They were later divorced.

I think I was depressed through most of my high school years. I slept a lot and missed school frequently. I even had a plan for alternating the days of the week that I stayed home—always with permission, of course. I would simply tell my mother before she would leave for work that I didn't feel well, and I would sleep most of the day. The next morning she would write a note saying I had been absent from school the day before because I wasn't feeling well. I never did it more than one day at a time, and always a Tuesday, Wednesday, or Thursday, never a Monday or a Friday. My mother never caught on, and I am surprised attendance counselors never questioned this behavior because I did it fairly often.

I don't remember my mother ever asking me about how I felt on these mornings, just like she rarely asked me where I was going and never when I would be back. She definitely never waited up for me at night. It was a good thing that I had good friends and I was not what you would call wild. However, there were times when I found myself in questionable places. I have always been so thankful that I never really got in trouble.

Graduation time came, and I was so glad to have this difficult chapter of my life come to a close. I dreamed of going to school somewhere completely new where no one knew me, where I could have a completely fresh start. But because money was very tight and I had a scholarship to the local state college, it was decided that I would go there.

My boyfriend agreed to go to the local community college to pacify his parents. He really did not want to go to college at all, resented education, and definitely did not apply himself. He lasted one semester then joined the service. It was during the Vietnam War, and he did not want to get drafted, so joining the service and going to Japan seemed like a safe way to both stay out of Vietnam and to get away from home.

Education was important to me, and I considered it my ticket to a better life down the road. It was important to me to get an education because I wanted my life to be better. Even though I was good at putting myself down, I knew I was not stupid. I wanted to go away to school, but it seemed like there was no way financially. Consequently, I became a commuter student in a school where sororities and fraternities abounded. I was too insecure to rush a sorority, and by this time I was developing a consciousness of the plight of the poor and the underprivileged. The poor and underprivileged were not the students in sororities and fraternities! I was beginning to question traditional middle-class values and the importance of status and impressions. So that first semester in college definitely did not meet the expectations of my dream. It was a lonely time, especially since many of my friends chose to identify with sororities. The feelings of aloneness only increased. Then came the final straw that sent me into the twilight zone.

My mother had been dating a man who was the farthest thing from my father. He was little and not athletic, he worked for the government, and he was missing his bottom front teeth. Can't you just see him? My father was big, athletic, talented, and had all of his teeth! My mother too was incredibly lonely. When the man asked her to marry him, she told him he would need to get his teeth fixed first.

They were married in August before my school started in September. I didn't like him, and my brothers liked him even less. But my brothers were gone—one on his own and married, and the other away at school on a track scholarship. They didn't have to live with him.

The straw that broke the camel's back came on a Saturday morning when my mother had been married to my "stepfather" (a word that I could hardly say at that time) for only five months. My brother's friend, whom I liked very much, was stationed with the army in the northern part of the state and was able to hitch a ride home one Friday night, about an eight-hour drive. My home was right along the interstate, so he asked to be dropped off by my house. I did not know he was coming, and I was out with friends. My car was parked in front of the house and unlocked. Since I was not home, he fell asleep in my car. In the middle of the night, I heard a tap at my bedroom window, and I invited him into my house. His home was about two miles from where I lived, and I told him I would take him home in the morning because it was very foggy. I gave him a pillow and a blanket and told him he could sleep on the couch in the living room. I then closed the doors to the hallway and to my bedroom and went back to sleep.

Early the next morning, my stepfather came storming into my room, demanding to know who the strange person was in the living room, and wanting to know why I had not gone into my mother's bedroom to tell her he was out there. For one, this person was not a stranger. My mother knew him well, and I was not about to go into my mother's bedroom where she was sleeping with her new husband. My stepfather proceeded to tell me that someone was going to leave, and it was not going to be him. He assumed something improper was going on, and I promptly told him that if I was going to do something questionable, I would have done it long before now, and I surely would not have picked my own home with others present to be the place.

Again my mother stood by, said nothing, and did not even acknowledge that she knew who the young man was. That was the beginning of the "twilight zone" part of my life. I left with my friend and told my mother I would be back for some of my things the next day. She told me that she knew I would be on my own soon and that she needed to think about her own life. She never asked me to stay, nor did she ask me where I was going. Until the day she died, she never knew where I went.

That morning we went to my friend's house. His mother was wonderful. We told her the situation, and she told me I could stay there as long as I needed to. The semester was ending at school, and I had a major paper to write. My friend went down to the beach with me, we sat on the rocks on the jetty, and he helped me finish my paper. He had been a student at a major university before he joined the army to avoid the draft. We went to Taco Bell for dinner (that was when everything at Taco Bell was nineteen cents each!), and then went to a movie.

When we got back to his mother's house, she had made a bed for me on the couch. What a difference. Needless to say, I liked his mother a lot. She loved kids, even teenage kids, and had an excellent rapport with her own young adult children. I could not help but think of the contrast between his mother's response and the response of my own mother. This woman put her arms around me, welcomed me, listened to me, and affirmed me, saying that she knew I would be okay, that God would take care of me. She was a woman whose life had been difficult, and she had learned to put her trust and her life in God's care. She inspired me, and I wanted to be like her when I was a mom, if I ever was.

The next day I went back home, packed up some of my clothes, called my great-grandparents, and asked if I could come and stay with them. I asked my mother for ten dollars so that I could get back and forth to school until I could finish the semester and get a job. She told me she thought I should learn to budget my money. I asked her how I could budget money I did not have. Reluctantly, she gave it to me. I never asked her for money again.

My great-grandparents were wonderful. They welcomed me with open arms and told me I could stay there as long as I needed to. They were eighty-six at the time.

# The Six-Year Courtship

We were just kids, both fifteen years old and sophomores in high school. I don't remember exactly how we met, but I do remember he was my first real boyfriend. He called me on the phone. He walked the two or three miles from his house to mine to see me, and sometimes he met me after class and walked with me to my next class. He kissed me and I liked it. It was nice to have someone show interest in me. We used to meet at the school canteen on Friday nights to dance and hang out. He would go with his friends, and I would go with mine.

I specifically remember one Friday night he scaled the wall at the canteen just as I was coming up the walk. He called down to me from the top of the wall and told me that he loved me. I said, "Tell me again when you are sober!" You see, life for him was about drinking beer on Friday nights and smoking cigarettes away from the controlling reach of his rigid, rejecting father.

He was not a happy person. He was quiet and secretive, and he had great difficulty communicating and talking about his feelings. He seldom showed any expression of emotion and rarely smiled. Maybe this was typical behavior for fifteen-year-old boys, but it seemed like he struggled with this more than most. I knew my own brothers didn't talk about feelings or even their thoughts, but then my home was pretty dysfunctional. How could I know what "normal" really was? All I knew was that he resented his father, did everything he could to keep from stirring the waters at home, and privately defied his father's expectations and resented his authoritarian rule.

He was the oldest of four children, with a brother just eighteen months younger, then another brother and sister ten and twelve years younger. As I mentioned earlier, his parents were well-educated, professional people. His father had great expectations for his oldest son.

I don't remember him taking me to his home that first year, although he would sometimes tell me to call him at home. When I did call his home, I would always tell his mother that he had told me to call. That was a generation when guys did the calling and initiated every contact, which was a whole lot different than teenage dating relationships today. I definitely did not want his parents to think I was chasing their son. He rarely answered the phone himself.

I was hungry for attention so I did just about anything he told me to do. He was smart, but he never really applied himself in school; he always did just the minimum to get by. I remember his father saying to me, "You would never know he had an IQ of 140." What a putdown. No wonder he resented his father.

During our junior year, he treated me terribly. It was the teenage year of my life I would like most to forget. He went out with other girls, many of them my friends. He'd spend maybe four weeks with one, then several weeks with someone else. This went on for most of the school year. He would call me from time to time, but he treated me awfully at school.

I had one class with him. Our desks and seats were connected by a post to the base of the metal frame. Somehow my seat had become disconnected from the post, and when I sat down, the seat fell off and I fell to the floor. It could have been very dangerous; I could have sat right down on that post. Ouch! And in those days, girls wore dresses to school. It was an awkward and very embarrassing situation. He thought it was so funny, he laughed right out loud. I was humiliated. Many years later, he did apologize and acknowledge that his response was very cruel. But the impact of his response is still with me today.

At Christmastime that year, I worked in a dress shop. A coworker introduced me to a friend of her boyfriend, who invited me to a New Year's Eve party. These guys were older, drove cool cars, and lived in another part of town that was far away from my own turf. My coworker friend went to another high school in the north part of the city. When I accepted the date, I did not know that these guys and their friends were a little more wild and crazy—actually a lot more wild and crazy—than me. I was really quite naïve. The guy, however, was very nice to me and treated me with respect when I declined the free-flowing beer and any sexual advances. We actually had some very good conversation, believe it or not. I think he sensed that I was a compassionate person and a pretty good listener, and he talked a little about his life. I think he wanted me to read between the lines and understand his addiction. It was not until several years later that I realized that several of these people, this guy included, were addicted to heroin and selling the stuff. I do believe God was looking out for me way back then.

I remember Mr. First Love calling me about one thirty in the morning on New Year's Day asking where I had been, why I was out so late, and who I had been with. I told him I had a date, and it really was not any of his business. I wondered why he was calling me. Why did he keep coming in and out of my life? Why did I care what he thought? Was I that desperate for attention? Sometimes I think, yes, I was lonely and would settle for any kind of attention. I am so grateful that I was not promiscuous. I was a tease, but I was adamant about not wanting to be used. When I look back, I can see again and again where I compromised my values and what was important to me just to receive a little attention.

Mr. First Love's relationship with me during this time was a little tricky because he needed me to help keep him out of trouble. Early in our relationship, he brought me his father's signature and asked me to write his absence notes and sign them with his father's signature when he chose not to go to school. I could imitate his father's signature fairly well. He would use the notes that I wrote rather than the real ones his father occasionally wrote for legitimate absences, and it was my signature that was on file in the attendance office. In our junior year he was in a little hot water because when he didn't go to school, he was not sure he could count on me to write his absence notes for him. Why should I do that for him when he had laughed at me so unmercifully and bounced around in relationships with my friends, one after another? Toward the end of the year, he skipped school and spent the day at the county fair. Then he came to me to write his excuse. I remember writing the note reluctantly, but I often wonder why I did it. Why would I compromise and give in to someone who treated me so unkindly? This was a question that haunted me for many years.

Somewhere toward the end of our junior year, he decided he liked me after all. We started dating regularly. On Friday nights he would go out with his friends, and then he and I would go out on Saturday nights. The dates were regular and always the same. We would either go to the drag strip and watch the races or go to the motorcycle races in a neighboring community. We would eat taquitos at the neighborhood Dairy Freeze, and occasionally he would invite me to his house. I hated the drag races and the motorcycle races, but what was I to do? If I complained, he would go without me. I guess I thought going to the races was better than sitting home alone. I guess I thought that was the best that I could do. I never dared to dream big dreams or wish for things that seemed so out of reach.

His family became like my own. I could talk to his mother, and his father liked me—a little too well. I babysat for his younger brother and sister on several occasions, and his parents even paid me to clean their house. It was almost like I became part of the family. Marg always told me she thought of me more like a younger sister than her son's girlfriend. His family included me in family events, and I have good memories of many special occasions. His family lived in one of the nicer homes in a more up-and-coming neighborhood than my own. I will never forget being at their house on the day that they received a new washer and dryer and had just had their kitchen completely remodeled. They showed me how you could cook bacon on a paper towel on a paper plate in just a minute or two. Amazing! It was the first built-in microwave oven I had ever seen, and I remember thinking that it must have cost a fortune. At my house, a new washing machine would have been a huge purchase, but a new washer and dryer and remodeled kitchen complete with a microwave, all at once, that was over the hill.

Mr. First Love did not shower me with gifts or compliments. In fact, he rarely gave me anything. He always had a job, so he did have spending money. He first worked for some local barbers, cleaning up the shop several days a week after school. I later found out that it was these young barbers who whetted his appetite for beer at a very young age. He went from the barber shop to washing dishes at a nice restaurant in the neighborhood. Throughout his senior year and until he joined the service, he worked at a gas station. So having spending money was not an issue for him. He just didn't share much of it with me. At Christmas he gave me a bottle of perfume that I treasured—an actual gift from him—only to be told later by Marg that it was a last-minute, "Mom, I need a gift" thing. It was something his teacher mom had received from one of her students—something she didn't want!

This story wouldn't be complete without prom night. Prom is when girls get all dressed up in formal wear, have their hair and nails done, and wait for Prince Charming to take them to a romantic dinner and a night filled with dancing and warm fuzzy memories, right? Well, not quite. It started off okay. We were all dressed up and went to dinner at a lovely restaurant, then we went on to the prom in a downtown hotel. I think I would be stretching it to say that we danced three dances. We left long before it was over and headed to meet up with "friends." He had not told me about this part of the plan until we were on the way. When we arrived at the motel, our "friends" turned out to be three other guys and a case of beer. Ah, but what a night to remember! I can't remember if there was one other girl there or not. I do remember just lying on a bed and feeling very alone. I think he took me home about two in the morning. That was my one and only prom experience. In the end, it did not make it to my list of top ten dates.

Summer passed, and we were both off to college. I received a scholarship and went to a local state college, and he was registered at the local city college. I said "I went" and he "was registered." That's correct. I went to classes to learn and prepare for my future. Though he was registered, he spent most of his time at the local slot car place racing miniature cars around a big track. He rarely was seen on campus and eventually dropped out before the failure notices came. Of course this was much to the consternation of his parents. They had such high expectations for him and were so disappointed in him and could not understand his behavior.

This was at a very traumatic time in our nation's history, a time when young men were being drafted and sent off to the rice fields of Vietnam to fight a senseless war. If you were male, over eighteen years of age, and not in school, you were sure to be drafted. Rather than being drafted and sent to Vietnam, Mr. First Love decided to join the navy (his father's alma mater) and head for Japan. We grew up in a navy town, and of all the branches of the armed forces, I disliked the navy the most. It's not that I was necessarily anti-military service at that time. My father had been in the army, my oldest brother in the US Coast Guard, and my second brother in the air force. It's just that we were taught to stay away from the navy base and the area of town that consisted of an amusement park, tattoo parlors, prostitutes, and bars that catered to sailors. Respectable girls did not frequent such places or the company of guys who did.

What I thought about the navy was the last thing Mr. First Love cared about. He cared most about not going to Vietnam, and this seemed like the best way for him to secure the next two years of his life and stay alive. So, off to the navy he went. That was during the twilight zone of my life, a time when I was on my own and trying to figure out what was important to me. He and I fought a lot, and his inability to communicate always seemed to precipitate arguments. I wanted so much out of life. It seemed like he had no hopes, no dreams, and no aspirations. We were so very different, and yet there was something that drew us together.

During the time that he was in Japan, his family became closer to me than ever. His parents even offered to have me live with them so that I could stay in school. That seemed so very generous of them, but I felt I could not accept their offer. Little did I know then that his family was almost as dysfunctional as my family. I was still so young and naïve. I do remember Marg saying to me that her oldest son (Mr. First Love) "was a nice guy, but he would never shake the world." She continually encouraged me to let her introduce me to other guys, people with more potential. I cannot imagine saying that about any of my own children. I felt bad for him that he could never meet the expectations of his parents, and they never had a clue what was inside of him. Actually, I don't think he really had a clue either. He was just angry and filled with resentment, but he appeared to be so passive, always protecting himself from getting caught and keeping it all very tightly tucked away deep inside of him.

We agreed that I would date others while he was in Japan. The more guys I met, the more I realized that I wanted so much more out of life than he did. I was energetic, loved life, and realized the value of communication. Although we had both been wounded in dysfunctional families, we responded to that wounding in very different ways. I wanted to talk about feelings; he did not. I was adventurous and wanting to try new things; he was not. I was active and athletic; he was not. I wanted to learn about different ethnic groups and cultures; he thought he was of the superior race. I had compassion for the poor and oppressed; he did not. I valued education; he did not. I wanted to explore the world; he wanted to stay put and do nothing. What drew us together? Not much.

The longer he was gone, the more I realized that I could not spend my future with him. There was a whole world to experience, and I was eager to learn and grow. I continued to write him letters and his letters became more and more affectionate. He talked about marriage and things he was bringing back for "our home": china, silverware, knives, bedding, etc. You know that saying about absence making the heart grow fonder. I think this was definitely a factor in the content of his letters. I never wrote to him about guys I had met or any of my dates during the time he was in Japan.

I remained very close to his family, and I think everyone expected us to marry. The longer he was gone, the more I realized that I could not marry him. This became very clear to me about six months before he returned home from Japan. I decided to wait until he returned home and tell him in person. And that is what I did.

# The Twilight Zone

The "twilight zone" was that three-year period in my life between the time I left home at the age of eighteen and the time I blindly left everything I had ever known at the age of twenty-one to get married in a foreign land to a man I barely knew.

Life in the twilight zone was filled with adventure, lots of new experiences, and special moments. It was a time in my life when I finally started to think about who I was, what I wanted in life, and what was important to me. It was also a time of compromise, a lonely time of survival, and a time of spiritual reflection.

My world suddenly became much bigger. I was exposed to people who were different than me and people from different cultures, from different economic classes, and different value systems. It was my exposure to life in the real world. I had a full-time job. I was responsible for my own food and shelter. I was on my own.

In many ways it felt like I had been thrown into this big ocean where I would either sink or learn to swim. Now you know there are all kinds of swimmers; there are those who dog paddle and there are Olympic swimmers. Believe me, many times it was all I could do to dog paddle or just tread water. On more than one occasion I took a gulp of that nasty saltwater then took my time spitting the taste of it out of my mouth. Do you know that experience? Maybe you would rather just forget it? I am still learning how to swim in this sea of life in a way that enables me to not only survive and keep from sinking but to be victorious, to win the race, and to reach the goal to which I have been called. I was not always so focused, so motivated to become the whole person that I was created to be. I was needy and wounded and alone much of the time during the years in the twilight zone. Reminisce with me now about some of those experiences and see if you recognize yourself.

Soon after I was on my own, Mr. First Love went to Japan. We agreed that I would be free to date while he was gone. I later realized that all the while he was in Japan, he was assuming we would marry when he returned. The longer he was gone, the more sure I became that I would not marry him. I wanted so much more out of life than he ever desired. I cared deeply for him, but there were too many differences and very little common ground. I guess the most common ground was that we were both wounded and needy. Somehow that did not seem like enough reason to marry.

In recent years, Mr. First Love has given me a folder full of letters to read, letters that he had written to his parents during his tour in Japan. Why now, after all these years, especially since he chose more than forty years later to leave our marriage to live with the girlfriend with whom he had lived for more than eight years? His mother had kept the letters for more than forty years and then sent them to him to do with as he pleased. I read through all of them. I was shocked as I read that he clearly told his family of his plans to marry me, that he considered me a part of his family, and that he appreciated that his parents had welcomed me and were "looking after me." For someone who seldom talked about his feelings, this was quite an eye-opener. He could say "I love you" to me, but he could not reveal any of his thoughts or show much emotion.

I knew even when I was young that it would be difficult to deal honestly with the marriage issue once he returned home from Japan, but I was committed to not doing anything to end the relationship until he returned. I always thought a "Dear John" letter was a cruel thing to do, and I really did care about his well-being. I would cross that bridge when he returned. Thus began my journey into adulthood.

As soon as the semester was over, I started my first full-time job at the telephone company. I had heard that anyone could get a job there, so that was the first place I went. I became employed full time as an information assistance operator, a job that was long ago replaced by technology. There were many single young women working there, and even though it was a crummy job with poor pay and hours, I liked the people with whom I worked. I worked a split shift so I could work in the morning, go to the beach in the middle part of the day, and then go back for another four-hour shift from five to nine in the evening. At first it barely paid for expenses, and there was no money to spare.

Okay, it's confession time. I carried this memory and guilt for way too many years and now I can't believe that I am really putting it in print, but somehow I feel that I may not have been alone. I also know that I was long ago forgiven. My roommate and I once ran out of toilet paper before payday, and it was a desperate situation. I stole a roll of toilet paper from a neighborhood gas station! I knew it wasn't right, but what else could I do? I was one of those people who never broke the rules for fear of punishment. Somehow I think God understood. As I look back now, it seems pretty trivial and humorous, but believe me, it was not at the time.

I did well as an information assistance operator and was offered a promotion. The only glitch was that to be promoted to a refer clerk, I had to be able to type. That was a serious problem. Being a refer clerk was such an exciting job, such an opportunity! You typed a list of current phone numbers in one column and the new, changed number in a second column. This list of changed numbers is what operators used to respond to callers when a number had been changed. They would say, "That number has been changed; the new number is…" Can you imagine doing that eight hours a day, forty hours a week? It was promotion, and I was an overachiever, so I wanted it. Most importantly, the pay was better.

But I couldn't type very fast. So I borrowed an old manual typewriter (there were no electric typewriters in that day), checked out a typing manual from the library, and practiced and practiced and practiced. It was a major sacrifice to forfeit some of my beach time, but if I wanted to be successful, I knew a little sacrifice might be required.) All the effort paid off. I barely passed the typing test, but I got the promotion and officially became a refer clerk.

So I began my journey to my promising career as a refer clerk. It paid for food, rent, car payments, and insurance, so it was okay for about two years. Imagine typing two columns of numbers forty hours a week just to be able to keep from stealing toilet paper. Back then I was not much of a dreamer; I just lived in the real world as best I could. I am grateful that I can dream bigger dreams today, but still, in many ways, I pretty much live in the real world. I am most grateful, however, that I have been able to find peace and joy in the midst of the real world.

I first moved in with another girl from work. That lasted about three months. When she informed me she was moving back home, I rented a studio apartment with a pull-down Murphy bed and lived alone for a few months. It just so happened that the girl in the apartment next to me was a friend of my brother and a few years older than I. She grew up in my neighborhood, and I liked her. We decided to pool our resources and share an apartment together. We got along well. We had different circles of friends, so we did not really do things together socially, but that worked out well.

She had a good-paying civil service job with the county and good hours. She encouraged me to take the county test. Because I had to work weekends, I had some weekdays off, which gave me the opportunity to take the county test during the week. My typing skills had greatly improved, and by this time I was pretty tired of typing refer numbers. Two years of that was enough! I was afraid of test-taking, but my roommate assured me that the test was easy enough that you did not need to be a rocket scientist to pass it. I thought I was at least as bright as she was, so why not go for it? I guess there were some benefits to working weekends, like those days off during the week when you can apply for jobs that normal people have from eight to five Monday through Friday. Once you passed the test, you were automatically placed on a list for open positions in the county, and then you just waited. It was only a matter of time until you would be placed. It was a huge county, so you needed to specify the area in which you wanted to be placed.

I first started to work for the Bureau of Public Assistance in a city about twenty-five miles away, but later I transferred to my own town, just a fifteen-minute drive from my apartment. I was actually hired as a transcriber to type case histories for forty hours a week. I am happy to say that I now type much faster than the mandatory forty words a minute, and the content is far more interesting than two columns of numbers. What is amazing, however, is after all that time typing numbers, I never memorized the number keys on the keyboard and still have to look at them on my computer today.

That pretty much tells you about how I supported myself during life in the twilight zone—except for one very significant detail.

When I transferred as a transcriber to my own city, I worked for the Department of Adoptions. I loved my work. It was a happy place where prospective parents could realize their dreams, a place where wounded, unwed birth mothers could find peace about the placement of their newborn infants into good homes. The caseworkers cared about their clients, both the prospective parents and the mothers, and they offered the precious newborns hope for a good life. I liked the people with whom I worked. So life was good!

This was a very unique era in American history. Think peace, not war, and love, love, love. I was an idealistic flower child who knew how to stuff the pain, wear a smile, and pretend. I actually thought of myself as a Pollyanna who never got mad. Was I ever in for a big-time revelation.

Among the interesting information in the letters I mentioned above was Mr. First Love's reference to my many moves. I think he even referred to me as a gypsy of sorts. All of the moves were unplanned, but I think there were about seven in two years. My first roommate moved home. Then I was alone. Then I got a new roommate, and we moved to a two-bedroom furnished apartment about two blocks away. Then we decided to save money and move to a less expensive unfurnished apartment in a not-so-nice neighborhood.

Save money we did, but the not-so-nice neighborhood proved to be an environment where two young and naïve women did not belong. During our stay at this humble abode, our landlord, who lived downstairs beneath our apartment, was beaten and severely disabled by an unidentified intruder. We never did find out what really happened, but we were sure there was much more to the story than we were being told. Shortly after that event, I had a visit from my New Year's Eve date, the heroin addict, who had just been released from prison. He told me that I should not be living in that area—this was where he used to come to buy his heroin.

By this time I was thinking I really would like to live closer to the beach anyway, and the timing seemed right to move again. We found a wonderful two-bedroom apartment in an older home down by the beach, and we both loved it. I thought I would stay there forever. But one morning I was getting ready for my split shift at the telephone company when I realized that my roommate was still there and using the bathroom. It was a weekday, and she was usually gone by the time I needed to get ready for work. I needed a mirror, and she had a large mirror on her dresser in her bedroom, so I just decided to use that. It was only as I was standing in my underwear in front of this large mirror that I noticed the reflection of the male body in the bed behind me! This was not a good start to the day. I was a very modest person and not at all comfortable standing in the presence of anyone in my underwear, much less a guy. I was mortified. My roommate and I had a discussion. I said that if it happened again, I would have to move. Little did I know that this had been going on for some time. He would park his truck around the corner and down the street. Since we worked different shifts, I rarely saw either one of them, except on an occasional weekend when I did not have to work. Needless to say, it did happen again and, you guessed it, another move. I loved this apartment and wanted to stay there, but I couldn't afford it by myself. I was heartsick. And to think that I had paid my half of the first month's rent there with money I had saved from my piggy bank, all seventy dollars. (In those days I saved only quarters in my piggy bank and bought a roll of quarters every payday.) We remained friends, but I could not bear the thought of another encounter with her boyfriend and me in my underwear, so what else could I do but move one more time? I did forgive her and later was a bridesmaid in their wedding.

So what do you think? Was I really a gypsy?

The last apartment was smaller but very close to the water in a wonderful neighborhood where many people wished they could live. It was pushing my budget at eighty dollars a month, but by this time I was working for the county, and I was able to do it. The apartments were in the back of a storefront building, and there were a number of single, young people living there. You could be with people if you wanted company, or you could be in the privacy of your own apartment if you wanted to be alone. I liked the other single people in the building and was delighted to have found this treasure. This was my home when I met Body Mind and Spirit. This was my home when I said good-bye to Mr. First Love. This is the environment that I left behind as I traveled to that foreign land to become the runaway bride.

You must wonder where my family was during these gypsy years. My oldest brother lived in Alaska, and my second brother served two terms in Vietnam in the air force. Though my mother and her husband lived across town, I had very little contact with them. I only remember my mother initiating a call to me on one occasion, so we seldom talked on the phone. I do remember her coming to one of the first apartments to bring me a hairdryer for my nineteenth birthday. Because I did not have a hairdryer, I would go to the Laundromat late at night on the edge of a not-so-nice neighborhood and sit under the coin-operated salon-style hairdryer. Because it was late, there were never any people in the Laundromat. Think about it: I was an eighteen-year old girl alone in a lit-up Laundromat late at night in a bad part of town. I told you I was naïve.

Occasionally I would wash my car at my mother's house. Other than that I do not recall that she ever came to visit me. It was Mr. First Love's family who showed me love and welcomed me into their home. I went to church with them and ate around their table, and they treated me like their own. Well, almost like one of their own.

Jack, Mr. First Love's father, showed me a little more attention than he did his children and thankfully not as much as he did his wife, but it was definitely more than was appropriate. I think I mentioned earlier that Mr. First Love's parents were professional people. I naturally expected them to act like responsible adults.

Having grown up in a pretty dysfunctional family, my role models for happy marriages were few and far between. And because I was very naive and only fourteen when my father died, I was pretty clueless about much of the facts of life. However, when Jack approached me in my bed to kiss me goodnight and tuck me in like he did the other children when I was staying at their home while Mr. First Love was home on leave, can you imagine my surprise when he laid himself out flat on top of my body and proceeded to kiss me with his tongue in my mouth? Seemed pretty strange to me, but what did I know? I didn't think this was normal, but how did I know what normal was? When he did it the second night, my concern grew, but I didn't say a word to anyone—not even to Mr. First Love.

I later learned, with the help of an excellent counselor, some of the reasons for a lot of the confusion in my life. I was closer to my father than my mother even though he beat me, but it was because he showed me affection. My mother showed little or no affection. Usually the person who shows you affection is not the one who abuses you. Did Jack just have a strange way of showing affection? Little did I know! The bedtime kisses were one thing, but the next incident was blatant and clear. Even I knew it was way out of bounds.

Mr. First Love's brother had his wisdom teeth pulled, and he needed ice bags to keep the swelling down. I offered to go to the store to get the ice bags. Jack suggested that he should go along as well. As I was behind the wheel of my little Volkswagen bug in route to the pharmacy for ice bags, Jack reached over and started fondling my breast. I pulled back in shock and said something dumb like, "I'm not used to having anyone touch me like that." I don't remember what he said, but I know I was glad when we got to the store. I don't remember any other conversation about that incident. Of course, I never told anyone about it until more than thirty years later. Surely I must have done something to encourage that behavior, and I needed to be very careful about what I did and keep my distance from Jack. He acted as though nothing had happened. Can you imagine a high school principal getting away with such behavior today? How many other young, innocent desirables had he touched?

Until the day he died, this man had a fetish for breasts. He declared he could see little or nothing as a result of his macular degeneration up until the day he died, but only a few short months before his death, he greeted me from across the room and then whispered in my ear, "Nice boobies!" And of course, he always wanted a close, tight hug. He also tried to fondle his granddaughter in the presence of her young son just a short time before his death. One of the fatherly words of wisdom he imparted to his sons was that they should be sure to marry women with nice breasts.

Forgive me for getting a little distracted. I guess recalling those events that shaped my life so many years ago brought back some recollections I would prefer to forget. Our definition of family definitely becomes distorted by unfortunate experiences we often keep hidden deep in our being. All I can say is that I will be forever grateful for God's love and protection and for God's loving hand upon my life, especially during those late nights under the hair dryer in the Laundromat.

Life in the twilight zone was interesting, to say the least; there was never a dull moment. I wanted so much but understood so little. I wanted to give love but really did not know how. I tasted love, but it could not be mine. My definition of love was confused with my insatiable need to be loved, and it has taken me many, many years and a lot of wise counsel to understand the true meaning of unconditional love. What a freeing thing it is to know the unconditional love of God and to be able to love another person unconditionally with no strings attached. What a world this would be if all humankind could experience these two realities.

The twilight zone in my life spanned three short years, but its impact will stay with me forever.

# Body, Mind and Spirit

Oh, to have known then what I know today!

He came into my life quite unexpectedly in the last year of the twilight zone. He was talented and smart and deep. I am amazed today at the impact he has had on my life. Now, almost fifty years later, the bond is greater than ever before. He would never be mine nor would I be his, but the bond between us will always be there.

It was a turbulent time in the world. There was much dissension in our country and around the world. The civil rights movement in the US was in full swing, and finally persons of color were demanding respect. The embers from the Watts riots in Los Angeles were still burning, and I was keenly aware of the injustice and prejudice so prevalent in society at that time. I was a flower child, thinking love and not war, and believed in the value of all persons and their God-given worth.

He was black. I was not. He was a musician with a beautiful voice. He knew what he wanted and where he wanted to go. He had dreams, and he wasn't afraid to follow them. I was naïve, wounded, and afraid to fail.

Friends took me to hear him play at a local night spot around the corner from where I lived. He was gifted, and I loved to listen to him play classical guitar. His voice was crystal clear. The year before I met him, he had returned from a year abroad as part of a USO hootenanny group. He had graduated from college and was in his first year of law school; he was supporting his education through his music. I only learned many years later that he had had quite a successful music career. His band even played on *The Tonight Show Starring Johnny Carson.*

I really don't know how it happened that he became my personal friend and soul mate. I just know that he opened the world for me. The attraction was mutual. He was all the important things: smart, educated, spiritual and deep, athletic, very talented, and handsome. We will call him Body, Mind, and Spirit (BMS). I asked him what attracted him to me, and he said it was my smile and my legs. I don't know about the legs, but the smile still has significance today. The legs still work, but I doubt they look the same.

He used to sing a song that said, "Think love and wear a smile." As a Christian today, that message still remains in my heart, and if I could only communicate one thing in my life, that would be a pretty good message. The song also said, "Our day will come." I had forgotten that part. Our day did not come. I am not sure why. However, some parts of our day will be with me forever.

He had been dating someone for many years, but when I met him, his longtime girlfriend had sent him packing. My longtime boyfriend was in the navy in Japan. I was becoming increasingly aware of the differences between us, and I think when I was honest, I knew that we were not a good match. My friends and I continued to go every week to hear BMS sing and play guitar.

Then came his first telephone call. We talked for what seemed like hours. Our telephone conversations continued, and I found myself amazed that we could talk about so many things. We both had a deep spiritual nature and could talk about the spiritual dimension of life. I had never had a relationship with a guy who was so sensitive, affirming, knowledgeable, motivated, and deeply spiritual. He had a positive approach to life and was not afraid to spread his wings. I was not a risk-taker. He was not afraid of failure. He had dreams, and he had the inner confidence needed to go after his dreams. Today he would say he was driven. I think his family would not have defined this as a positive attribute in the years to come.

He lived in the big city a little distance away. We talked on the phone often, and I began seeing him every week when he came to work in my neighborhood. By this time he was beginning to draw quite a regular group of fans. Although he had a connection with his fans, he wanted me to know my connection with him was different. He did not want me to get to know any of the guys who came to hear him sing and play guitar. He made me feel special, and he would always come to my apartment when he was finished with his gig. We would talk for hours, and each time we talked, it seemed my world would get bigger. He wanted to teach me about life, and I wanted to learn. I was so naïve. He wanted to teach me about other cultures. He wanted to expose me to a world far greater than I had ever experienced. He had traveled the world, and although he had been raised in the "traditional" black family of that day, he somehow had the confidence and the drive to step out of that mold and soar like an eagle. His voice and his talent had been his ticket to a new world, and he was not about to settle for less than the mountaintop. He was such an inspiration to me, with my low self-esteem and fear of failure. I wanted so much too, but I just didn't know how to make it work. He was intelligent and was committed to doing whatever it took to get that law degree.

I always thought of myself as a tomboy, so seeing myself as an attractive young woman with any sexual appeal just did not compute. My goodness, I needed a lot of education in this area. I was so naïve that I really did not have a clue about what sexy was. On one occasion he had planned an educational evening for me in the big city. When I asked him what I should wear, he said I should wear something sexy. Since I made most of my clothes, I decided I should make something special for this occasion. I have to chuckle now when I think about my definition of "something special." I made a silky black dress—sounds like a good start, doesn't it?—with a high turtleneck and sheer, black long sleeves. It was an A-line style that kind of fit like a tent. It was a good thing he liked my legs because they were the only things that were showing. Skirts were fairly short then, so that may have been the only thing that saved the evening. He was very kind and never said a word about my tent, but I am sure this was not what he had in mind.

In spite of my special tent, the evening was wonderful. He showed me things in the city I had never seen. He took me to meet his brother and his French wife and their beautiful children at their home. He took me to dinner and treated me like a queen. What a different world this was from drag races and motorcycle races. I wanted more of this life!

He kissed me like I had never been kissed before. He touched me like I had never been touched before. When we were together, it was as if we were one. We were connected body, mind, and spirit.

On one occasion some of our friends and I went to an after-hours club in the city to hear a trio of three young women whom he had been coaching. He met us there and was so proud of the girls. They were talented and showed a lot of promise. It was there that I saw Lou Alcindor (later to become Kareem Abdul-Jabbar) for the first time in person while he was still a college student. I was standing just a few feet away from him and was envious because he had such a good view of the girls. I thought he was standing on a box. Then I realized that he had such a good view because he was seven feet tall.

From this after-hours club, we went to BMS's home for breakfast. I will never forget the look on his mother's face when she came into the kitchen to see her son making breakfast for three white people—two blonde girls and a guy. I told you he had broken out of the traditional mold. His mother was a "domestic" for wealthy entrepreneurs and was content with this being her "proper place" in life. How could it be that he was her son—educated, talented, driven, and integrated? It was not until many years later that he told me that his mother did not like me because she was afraid he would marry me.

Spring turned to summer, and he and I had many more conversations. I helped him buy his favorite acoustic guitar, which later brought him an abundance of accolades and plenty of the necessities of life. Although we talked about our other relationships from time to time—that is, my relationship with Mr. First Love and his relationship with his longtime girlfriend, who decided she wanted him back—the conversations became more serious as the summer went on. He asked if I was jealous of his longtime relationship with this young woman from another city. We did not talk about the nature of the relationship much, only that she was a teacher and he felt obligated to marry her. He had questions about the relationship but felt he did not have much choice. It was expected that he would marry her. I did not express jealousy, rather just the knowledge that that's the way it was and there was nothing I could do about it. So often that has been the way I have dealt with life. He said he was jealous of Mr. First Love because it was getting close to August, when he knew Mr. First Love would return. I assured him that I was not going to marry Mr. First Love, and that was very clear. Then came the hard part. BMS informed me that his wedding was scheduled for August.

In the meantime, Mr. Social Worker came to work in my office at the Department of Adoptions. He was a kind and gentle person, easy to talk to, educated, moral, and he took faith seriously. He was only working in our office for the summer. We began spending time together—lots of time together. He was nice. Life was getting complicated! BMS was getting married but still very much in touch. Mr. First Love was coming home. Mr. Social Worker was very nice, older, educated, moral, and very interested in me. In fact, he told me he wanted to spend the rest of his life with me. How could this be when he only came to work in our office in June, and I did not go anywhere with him until July? What was I going to do?

I told Mr. Social Worker that I could not tell him that I loved him. He said that was okay, that I would. That night I looked in the mirror and said "Why not?" And that was it. I met the bus when Mr. First Love came back to the States, spent a couple days with his family, then told him I was not going to marry him. I went to BMS and G's wedding a few days later—and then came the shock. BMS asked me to sign his marriage certificate as his witness. A part of me went with him and G as they began their new life together. I told him I was not marrying Mr. First Love and that I was leaving on the first of September to get married in a foreign land. On the day I left my home for the past twenty-one years, I went to the bank to receive the remainder of the money that I had loaned BMS for that beautiful acoustic guitar. I then headed across the country for a new life in a new land with people I did not know who knew nothing about me. This was a new start to what I hoped would be a better life with a memory of a very special connection buried deep in my heart.

# Runaway Bride

He came to town in the summer of 1967, between his two years of graduate school in social work. He came with another student just for the summer. They lived along the beach and shared a car. I worked for an adoption agency. He came to work there as an applicant parent worker as part of his internship work for his graduate school program.

The social workers were either applicant parent workers or child care workers. This was in the day before the Roe versus Wade decision, when an adoptive family could expect to wait only five to seven months for what they called a "matched Caucasian infant." When an applicant parent family was approved for adoption, the child care workers and the applicant parent workers would come together to what they called a "matching board." Together they would decide which child should be placed with which family based on the requests of the applicant parents and the information provided by the child care worker on the background of the infants available for adoption.

This was an historic time in the history of the United States. It was during the Vietnam War, and the hippie movement was alive and well. It was popular to think love, not war, and I was a Pollyanna of sorts. I actually thought I never got angry. (It was years later that I discovered, much to my amazement, that I was not filled with anger—I was filled with rage!) I too lived by the beach. I had a five-foot flower painted on my front door. I lived in the back of a storefront building in which there were several apartments, the majority of which were occupied by young, single, free-spirited friends. I was not wild, as were some in the building. However, I was wounded, lonely, and very naïve. When I would make spaghetti or cherry pies, I could count on my neighbors to come to the table. My longtime boyfriend was in the service in Japan in an effort to avoid the draft to Vietnam. Even though my mother only lived a few miles away, I had little contact with her. So I was alone, sort of unattached, and seriously questioning the roller coaster relationship that had been part of my life since I was fifteen years old. Then, when I was twenty-one, along came the social worker.

It all started with a ride home from work and a question about a swimsuit. I passed the apartment of my social worker friend on my way to and from work every day. Because he shared the car with his roommate, the social worker asked me if I could give him a ride home. On the way, he asked me if I thought it would be okay for him to wear his basketball shorts to the beach, since he did not have a bathing suit and could not get one until he received his first paycheck.

I might have been a flower child who believed in living simply, especially since I was somewhat rebellious in those days about my empty, shallow, middleclass upbringing, but impressions were still pretty important to me. I didn't really know what basketball shorts looked like. All I knew was that guys wore Hawaiian-print jams to the beach. I could sew, I had a pattern, and I knew where to get the material. I think I had made a pair for my brother. So, I suggested that maybe the basketball shorts would not be the best, but I would be glad to make him a pair of jams and bring them to him the following Saturday evening.

This might sound like a very generous offer from someone who had an interest in advancing the relationship. This was not my motivation. I think in that day I would have done it for anyone.

He thanked me, but he did not have money to pay for the material or my time. I told him that it was no problem and continued on down the road past his apartment on the way to the store where he was to pick out the material that he liked for his new jams. I really think he was beside himself. I think he had some preconceived ideas about life in a beach town, but he really couldn't believe that someone he barely knew would offer to make him a bathing suit and pay for the material on top of it.

He picked out the fabric. I bought it and then proceeded to take him back to his apartment. I told him that I would bring the swimsuit to him the next evening. I went home, cut out the jams, sewed them up, and appeared at his door toward evening the next day. I spent a lot of evenings at home by myself, so it really was not an imposition for me to sew up the jams that Friday night. I spent a lot of nights sewing, usually for myself. It felt good to do something for someone else.

When I appeared at his door the next evening, I think he was kind of shocked. I think it seemed really strange to his roommate who opened the door that I was standing there with a pair of jams that I had just made. I simply told him that I had the bathing suit for the other social worker, and I needed him to try it on.

I will never forget the look on the social worker's face when I told him he would need to come out of the doorway of the bathroom so that I could see how they fit. He sheepishly came into the room, extremely self-conscious in this new bathing suit. What I didn't know was that he had never worn a bathing suit that did not have a built-in athletic supporter. I didn't know much about athletic supporters, other than that my brother wore them to play basketball, so it wasn't an issue for me. It was not until sometime later that I realized that this was a major deviation from the norm for him. He did get used to the idea, however, and wore that pair of jams for twenty or more years. I can't remember if it was with or without an athletic supporter.

The social worker had come to the Department of Adoptions in June, and I made him a bathing suit that month, but I did not go anywhere with him until sometime after the first of July. He later told me that he was trying to decide whether he would ask me out or another person from our office. He said he was drawn to my smile, but maybe the jams had something to do with his decision as well. I still just thought of him as my friend. He took me to a movie, and then he kissed me.

I started spending every evening with him, and we talked, and talked, and talked. I had never really talked with anyone other than Body, Mind, and Spirit about the things that were deep in my heart. The social worker shared the same values that were important to me. He was several years older than me, was educated (which was very important to me), and took his faith very seriously. He was an excellent listener and a trained counselor. Because I had come from an abusive home, he seemed to understand when I talked about my feelings, and he was incredibly supportive. He seemed to understand the devastation in my life—my out-of-control father, finding my father dead at the age of fourteen, the rejection by my stepfather, and then what seemed to me to be the rejection by my mother as well when I was eighteen. He told me that all of the things I shared that were important to me were characteristic of a Christian life. I think I had always been sensitive to spiritual things, but the only place I had experienced Christianity in action was in the "Raggers Ceremonies" in my YMCA camp experience. These were very personal, spiritually directed group experiences that were an integral part of the YMCA camp program. I went to church, but either the message was never spoken or I just didn't hear it. I had never really heard a message of salvation.

Although I was not physically drawn to him, he seemed a safe place for me. Little did I know then that what I was drawn to was a gentle father figure.

Sometime that August, I was shocked when I heard him say something like, "I am ready to spend the rest of my life with you." Was he asking me to marry him? I hardly knew him. That night, after he was gone, I looked into the mirror. I recalled that as a teenager I used to lie in my bed at night praying that if only someone would love me, I could do just about anything. I used to think a lot about just going somewhere new, leaving everything behind, and starting my life over. This was my opportunity. It was a clear and defining moment. As I looked in the mirror, I said to myself, *Why not? He is kind, moral, educated, and he shares my values. He has a master's degree, so he should be able to provide for a family, and he wants me.* What was so hard about that decision? Certainly what he was offering me was far better than anything I had ever known. Surely this should be safe. Why wouldn't I say yes? It had nothing to do with love, but it had everything to do with a lot of need. It just made good sense. He would love me, and I would be whatever he needed me to be. Far worse tradeoffs had been made.

So the next day at work, I called his extension and asked him to meet me in an empty office. I said I had thought about his offer and wanted to talk about it. We talked briefly and agreed to go down to the beach and talk further after work. I think he was a little surprised by my quick response, and I kind of caught him off guard. He wanted to make sure I was sure. He said that he had stopped looking for a wife on his own terms and believed God would let him know when the right person came along. I told him I couldn't tell him that I loved him, but he assured me that it was okay, that I would in time.

My longtime boyfriend returned home from Japan the first week in August. He thought he was coming home to his bride-to-be. I had known for several months that I was going to end the relationship, but I did not want to write him a "Dear John" letter when he was so far away. I felt that I needed to talk to him in person, so I arranged to pick him up at the bus station and go with him to his parents' home, which was like home to me. His family was my family, too. I then told his mother that I was not going to marry him and that I was moving away to marry my social worker friend. She didn't have any problem with my not marrying her son. She was always trying to fix me up with other people, saying that "her son was a nice guy but was never going to shock the world." However, she was disappointed my groom-to-be was a social worker because they "didn't make much money." That seemed the least of my worries then.

Saying goodbye was difficult for me, since I had been part of my boyfriend's family for six years. During the two years that he was in Japan, my boyfriend's family treated me like their own. I actually saw much more of them than I did my own mother. They included me in all their family activities, and I knew that they cared deeply for me. I spent three days with them and then finally, painfully, told my boyfriend that I was leaving. He was devastated. He had always assumed that I would be there and that we would live happily ever after. It was a very emotional time for me.

The understanding was that I would say goodbye then meet my soon-to-be fiancé at his apartment. These were the days before cell phones, and there was no way my fiancé could know when I was coming. I parked the car down the street and started to run toward his apartment, and he came running toward me at that very moment. I felt so safe and understood. This was a happy moment, a moment filled with promise and opportunity—finally, an opportunity to experience a good life. I was more than ready to go.

We left the first of September in my Volkswagen bug packed with most of my earthly belongings and two sleeping bags. The rest of my things were packed in boxes and sent ahead in a commercial truck. I turned my apartment over to a friend from work, complete with all of my furnishings, meager though they were. Thus began a twenty-five-year chapter in my life.

We spent eleven days driving cross-country, sleeping under the stars and cleaning up in gas station bathrooms or campgrounds. We first went to see my brother who was in the air force and introduced him to my husband-to-be. We then went on to meet the family of my soon-to-be brother-in-law. To this day, these are exciting memories. Once I left, I never looked back, never questioned what I was doing or whether it would work; that is, not until twenty-five years later. I even remember my stepfather saying to my mother, "Does she know what she is doing?" and my mother said, "I think she does." Did I? Who knows? I just knew it had to be a better life than anything I had ever known, and I was going for it for all I was worth.

As we traveled, I learned a lot about him. He had grown up with some of his own pain. He came from an extremely poor family that had experienced judgment, of all things, from wealthy members of his church because of his family's poor economic status. In his early years he felt somewhat inferior at school. He told the story of the humiliation he experienced when a skunk had sprayed his home. The family had no bathtub or shower (no indoor plumbing), although they tried the best they could to rid themselves of the smell. The children went to school, were isolated from the other children, and then were sent home because they smelled so bad.

I believe some of the painful stigma of poverty still lives with him today, although he has overcome so much. He has always had compassion for the poor and oppressed. That rang so true with me. He talked about his being quiet and how important it was to him to be accepted in his quietness. I was much more outgoing. He talked about his own self-esteem and how important it was to be affirmed and never put down in the presence of others. I learned early on how important it was to never undermine him, especially when we were with friends. This seemed so right.

I later learned that his parents' relationship was not so healthy. His mother, Anna, was quite simple but very kind in her own way and was always sustained by her deep faith. His father, George, was bright, but I thought he was insensitive to the needs of his wife. George was always kind to me, but I was often saddened by the way he treated his wife. I was always amazed, however, that George, with only an eighth-grade education, inspired all of his five children to go to college. All have graduated from college, and four have master's degrees.

After eleven nights under the stars, including one under a park bench covered with bugs because it rained and one on the banks of a reservoir in a public park in the middle of Topeka, Kansas because we could not find any campgrounds there, we arrived at our destination where my husband-to-be needed to start school the second week in September. He and his roommate of two years shared a two-bedroom apartment, and they made a bed for me on the floor in the second bedroom.

In the first week I found an apartment of sorts for all of $73 per month and then found a job that paid $2.24 an hour, less than half of my previous hourly wage. I had brought about $1,000 in savings with me, so I had money for rent and a car payment. Then my husband-to-be told me that he needed money for his tuition for this new term. Of course I gave it to him. In the weeks ahead, I met some of his family members, witnessed the extreme poverty of his parents, experienced a lifestyle that was completely foreign to me, and set a wedding date for October.

Two weeks after I arrived in my new home, my fiancé received his field placement assignment in another city about two hours away, where he needed to stay three days out of every week. Here I was in a new place, not knowing a soul. I only knew the way to and from my apartment to my place of work. I had every opportunity to turn around and go back to the land from which I had come, but it never entered my mind. I was starting a brand-new life, a life without pain and rejection, safe from violence, with someone whom I could trust.

In the weeks ahead, I focused on my new job and the details of my wedding. I made my wedding dress with the help of the pastor's wife. When the wedding day approached, my mother and grandmother came. My air force brother came to give me away. (I always joke about the fact that my brother was annoyed because he had to take his hand out of his pocket for this occasion. He rarely showed emotion and definitely not affection!) I really only knew three people at my wedding besides the groom. It was a small wedding, but since there were fifteen brothers and sisters on Anna's side of the family and weddings were the thing to attend, the small church was not too empty. Thus began the journey.

I will tell you today, it was probably the best thing that happened in my life. I will be forever grateful that it was in this chapter of my life that I came to know a loving, personal relationship with my Savior and Lord, my very best friend. I also have three wonderful children as a result of this union, and the social worker continues to be a good friend.

# The Journey

When I think about that first year, my mind is filled with vivid memories. I know without question that there must have been times when my husband wondered what in the world he had gotten himself into. For me, however, it was about learning what worked and what did not. After all, if I was going to have this better life, then I would need to learn how to live in it.

I said that I was much more outgoing than he. I soon became aware that in social situations I needed to take a back seat so that he could feel comfortable in his quietness. I always tried to involve him in the conversation and ask his opinion rather than stating mine, etc. I helped him to feel comfortable.

Very early on I mentally took note of all the comments in order to be a good, supportive Christian wife. I don't remember talking much about these things, but they made powerful impressions on my inner being, and I never forgot them.

One evening after dinner and a delightful evening of card playing at the home of another couple, my husband told me that it was not good for me to have sat across the table from the other woman's husband, even though she had seated me there. He said he noticed my eye contact with the other woman's husband. I just sat where they directed me and thought nothing of it. I thought you were supposed to look at people when you talked to them. Of course, this made me feel very uncomfortable. So much for a budding friendship with two very nice people. We never went to their house again, nor did we invite them to our home.

Then, several weeks later, the same discussion arose about me having eye contact with a salesperson in a furniture store. I know now that I didn't do anything wrong, but these incidents set me on a course that would profoundly affect the next twenty-five years of my life. Early on in my marriage, I was told not to say the word *darn*, especially in front of Anna. This was pretty foreign to me because I grew up in a home where *darn* was an ordinary word, and it was profanity that was not acceptable. In this family, *darn* was profanity. Please note that this was not a bad thing. I stopped saying it then and have never said it since, but it was just shocking to me at the time.

When I made my own dresses, they needed to be baggy and long, even though it was in the day of mini-skirts. Good Christian women were supposed to dress modestly and were not supposed to have short hair. I had had short hair most of my life. However, my hair was shoulder length when I got married—lucky for me! In fact, when I cut my sister-in-law's hair for the first time when she was seventeen or eighteen, Anna rationalized that because of where I came from, I didn't know any better. I think she even wrote in a letter to my husband before we were married something like, "Nothing good could come from where I came from."

Although she was always kind to me, I never felt emotionally close to Anna. While the other in-laws called her "Mom," I just could not do it. I didn't even call my own mother "Mom." I guess I just never felt like I was made out of the right mold.

However, I think Anna respected me for my new and growing faith, and I always tried to be helpful, especially at mealtime. In the days before there was running water in the house, it soon became my job (self-appointed, I think) to scrape and rinse the dishes, heat the water, and then wash them. I had never seen anyone work so subserviently and with so little recognition as my new mother-in-law. Helping with the dishes was the least I could do.

Then there was that ongoing thing about men. Did I know that it was not good for a woman to be a secretary because secretaries always got involved with their bosses? These were my husband's words, not his mother's. What was I to think? My mother had worked as a secretary to executive management for more than twenty years, and I knew she was never involved with her boss. How could I ever have gone to a male hairdresser for a haircut, even if the haircut wasn't short? My self-esteem and my identity were on a downward spiral to somewhere deep inside of me. One thing was for sure, though: there were rules in this new way of life, and I was going to have to learn to play by them.

I mentioned earlier that I had been a Pollyanna of sorts, that I thought I never got angry. Well, as I piled all of these mental notes in the back of my mind, I was fighting this control with all of my being. It seemed the only time my husband got angry was when I said he was trying to control me. I hate to admit it, but I threw more than one temper tantrum—I even shocked myself! You have heard that it is important when disciplining children to change the behavior but not break the spirit. I think this is when my spirit began to break, way back then. No wonder my husband later said that that first year was rough. It was rough for both of us. But we were idealistic and full of adventure, and I wanted to be the right kind of person and the right kind of wife. Thus I began the journey of hiding painful things deep inside of me, not talking about them, pretending everything was okay, pressing on to a better life. Because I hated conflict so much, I would do just about anything to avoid it. I equated conflict with violence. Pretending seemed to work, and my mother had taught me how to do that well. Unfortunately, my sense of humor, which was once alive and well, somehow got buried along with everything else.

Before I ever had children, I got the message loud and clear: support your husband, don't draw attention to yourself, don't look at men, especially in the eye, and look frumpy. Whether this message was intended or not, it was very clear. It definitely didn't do much for my self-image. I had grown up as a tomboy, tried to learn how to become feminine and feel good about myself, and even tried to understand what it meant to look "sexy," something I don't think I ever really accomplished. Now I was losing my identity altogether.

But I was serious about my faith. It was during this time that I was baptized and said publically that I now understood that Christianity was a way of life, not just going to church on Sunday. I was trying so hard to learn about this new and better way of life. Along the way, I placed self-imposed expectations on myself that my husband knew nothing about. He had his own expectations for a wife, which were significant enough. I didn't need to add my own sick ideas to the list of dos and don'ts. If I had been able to talk to him about my feelings, things might have been different. After all, he was a social worker and a trained counselor. But I did not talk about my feelings. I was afraid to touch any of those deep feelings, especially if I thought they conflicted with the new way of life, so I just continued to pretend they did not exist.

In those days we lived very simply in a little unfurnished two-bedroom house with a newly carpeted living room. My husband and I were both working then to pay off his student loans, and he was completing his obligation to the state for a stipend that he had received for graduate school. We made a kitchen table out of a door by cutting it off and screwing four legs onto it. Our bed was a mattress on the floor, and our dresser was a heavy old piece we had found in the attic. The extra bedroom was lined with bricks and boards, and lots of books and candles. In the living room there was my portable TV that I had brought with me, a pole lamp, and a high-back rocking chair that we had bought for twelve dollars deep in a Kentucky holler from the man who made it. We continued to work at paying off the school debt and moved temporarily to a furnished home of some church members in the rural community where my husband grew up.

In August of 1969, we moved again, this time so that my husband again could become a full-time student in a three-year seminary program. For the first six years of our marriage, I worked full-time; he worked two years and was in school and unemployed for four years. After the first year of seminary, we moved again closer to his childhood home, where he finished his last two years of seminary. I never really questioned the moves. He always felt led, and I wanted to be supportive. Altogether, we had moved eleven times in seven years. Living simply paid off when it came to moving.

By this time we were talking seriously about having a family. The school debts had been paid with my inheritance from my great-grandparents, and he would be employed full-time when he was finished with seminary. It was his turn to be the breadwinner. I had worked full-time for nine years and looked forward to staying home and raising a family. This was especially important to me, as I had memories of going to daycare before daycare was a household word. My mother worked outside of the home from my earliest memory.

When no children came after concerted effort, the doctor gave me a clean bill of health. It soon became clear that my husband had a fertility problem. The whole area of male infertility was relatively unresearched at that time, and doctors offered little encouragement. After a short time, we were encouraged to apply for adoption.

For some women this would have been a major hurdle. I can honestly say that for me, it was just another one of those things that I could not control. I had never had an intense need to carry or birth a child. It was harder for my mother. She had no problem accepting the children when they came, but she did have difficulty accepting that I would not have the experience of giving birth. Both my husband and I believed that God wanted us to be parents, and adoption was something we had talked freely about from the beginning. We had met at a county adoption agency, after all.

From the very beginning of the adoption experience, we had a good rapport with each other and our social worker. In fact, we first applied for a child through HOLT, an international agency, and needed to have a home study done by the local welfare agency. The local caseworker had never handled an international adoption, and my husband helped her through it.

We were approved by HOLT but then decided to pursue adoption options with a local agency in a larger neighboring city since overseas adoptions were considerably more expensive. We liked our caseworker, and we knew how to answer the questions. The caseworker asked us why we wanted to be parents and then set out to find us a baby.

It was at this time that the Roe versus Wade decision had just been handed down in the courts. Because of the legalization of abortion, what once took five to seven months for a Caucasian infant now took five years, and there was no such thing as a "matching board" where prospective parents' backgrounds and wishes were matched with newborn infants. We always thought it was a little funny that because of our religious affiliation we were not eligible for a Caucasian baby through this local agency. However, if we were interested in a minority child, they could help us because minority children were considered hard-to-place. And with hard-to-place infants, the policy did not apply. They said it had nothing to do with prejudice, it was just the policy of the agency. Little did they know that we were the lucky ones!

We had a decision to make. We knew God wanted us to be parents, so what kind of a baby did He want us to have? After further discussion, it became clear that the children available to us through this agency were biracial children of African American and Caucasian descent. Were we open to this? How would we raise them? What would we teach them about who they were? The decision was really not a difficult one for us.

I remember how grateful I was for my conversations with Body, Mind, and Spirit about how beautiful mixed-race children were and how they were a wonderful mixture of all that was good. I remember thinking how glad I was that I had had a personal relationship with more than one black person, and for my exposure, though somewhat limited, to the black community. My husband had also had positive experiences with black families and had an African American roommate.

What would we tell our children about their heritage? We would tell them that they were beautiful, that God made them just as he wanted them to be, and that He had a plan and a purpose for their lives. We would teach them about black history and make sure they had opportunities for interaction with others like themselves. We would teach them that people come in all colors, just as they come in all shapes and sizes, that all are valuable and made in the image of God. We would tell them everything we knew about their birth parents and hold nothing back so that there would be no surprises. We would treat them as our own flesh and blood, as gifts from God whom God had entrusted into our care. It would not be possible to love a child more.

I guess the caseworker liked what we said because six weeks later we received our infant son. He had blond hair and blue eyes, and was as fair as I am. What a glorious day! A gift he was, and a busy one at that. He was a happy baby boy, full of life and easy to love. I recall that prior to the placement, my husband had some apprehension about being able to show affection from day one, but when the day arrived, father and son were a team. Thank you, God! By the time he was about three, our son had a head full of beautiful blond curls.

That's when his sister came to us from the same agency. Our daughter's caseworker wanted us to have another child, but she asked a few more serious questions. This baby was not blonde and fair. She had black eyes, lots of straight dark hair, and beautiful olive skin. The caseworker had asked me how I felt about having "black, black" grandchildren. I told her that if I couldn't feel okay about that, then I should not have this child. Today I have a dark-skinned son-in-law and seven beautiful grandchildren. Three of my grandchildren are brown-skinned. I have two very fair daughters-in-law and four other very fair grandchildren, all with beautiful blonde curls just like the curls of my oldest son a long time ago. (Today he has no hair, curly or straight!)

Although we shared very little affection between us, my husband and I were both able to show affection to our children. We appeared to be a happy family. Our children received lots of love, and ours was a peaceful home. There was never any shouting or raised voices. My husband and I never fought, and we tried to teach our children the values that were so very precious to both of us. I do know that my husband felt that my response to him changed after the children came. I am sure that it was our faith in God and our commitment to our children that kept us together so long.

It was during this time that I began to feel very distant from my husband. He was gone nearly every night, often working late at the church. I remember having conversations with a friend about the meaning of love. I concluded that love was a way of life, not a feeling. I tried hard to convince myself. I later learned that my friend attributed these conversations to saving her own marriage. I am not sure how much they helped mine. At the time of our separation, my husband told me that he had considered filing for divorce many years ago, and I know it must have been about this time.

One night, very late, I awakened, looked down the hill at the church, and saw the light in the study was not on. I said to myself, *He must be down at the donut shop, or I am really stupid.* I don't think he was at the donut shop; I do know that I was very naïve yet very loyal. By this time, finances seemed tighter than ever, and it seemed there just was not enough money to go around. I was not a spender, and I was very resourceful. I did everything I could to conserve our resources. However, I knew very little about our finances other than that there wasn't much money and something had to give.

I began babysitting for a friend's child, and then I started watching both of her children. My husband offered me the opportunity to go back to school or to have another child. I chose to have another child. He said he noticed how much our children enjoyed the friend's toddler who had become part of our family; he decided another child would be good for us. Soon after this, however, he felt that it was best for me not to babysit anymore. It was causing problems in our family. He had spoken to the elders of the church about this, and they agreed that I needed to stop. How could I resist the counsel of the elders?

Our second son also came to us as an infant. Because he was born in the southern part of the state and because of his racial mixture, the agency felt it would be better for him to be placed in the north. Once again we were delighted. God had given us the most beautiful children in the world. In time there were eighteen adopted children in our congregation, and eleven of them were other than Caucasian.

We chuckle today about a conversation we had just before the arrival of our third child. My husband was leading a weekend retreat at a camp where some people began talking to us about adoption. I remember saying to my husband, "Did you tell them that the children were adopted?" He said, "No, did you?" Then we both looked at each other and said together, "Then how did they know?" I guess we forgot that all you had to do was look at them and know that they did not look like us. It just never occurred to us. And so it was, and still is today. They are ours, and we are theirs, and we and our grandchildren come in all sizes, shapes, and colors.

Even though inflation was high when our children were young. My husband found the land of his dreams, the "perfect place to raise a family." He had found temporary financing so that we did not have to have a construction loan. What good Christian wife would try to squelch such a dream? Not this one, although I had reservations from day one. We built a new home.

When our youngest son was two, our dire financial situation hit an all-time high. I knew I had to get a job. When the baby was five, I even took on a second job painting dorm rooms in the middle of the night at a local college where I worked just so that I could buy each child a special Christmas gift. I never had any money of my own, not even so much as an allowance. The debts increased, there was no money, and the financial situation worsened with each day. I worked during the day, my husband worked at night, and there was little or no interaction between us. My husband was becoming more and more dissatisfied with his work at the church and was inquiring about other pastorates. He finally challenged my administrator at work from the pulpit, and my job was reduced to less than full-time. Of course, I had to find another full-time job. The financial weight of the house was killing us, and I just wanted out. I thought that if we could just sell the house, our financial troubles would be over, but that was only the surface of a pile that was too long buried—a volcano that was about to erupt.

All during this time, I was beginning to lose weight without trying. Just the smell of food made me sick. My world was coming unglued. I just kept pretending that it would get better, but it didn't.

Finally, the house sold, and we moved into an apartment that my husband selected, one I had never even seen until the day we moved in. He had quit his job at the church after resigning on a Sunday morning and soon started another church. I had lost my home, my job, and my friends and family from the church, and I was wasting away. I needed healing and help.

When I finally decided on separation, I felt some relief. I told the new church that I had been a failure as a wife, as a mother, and as a friend, and I was going to get some help. We had been to several counselors, but things did not get better. I began to see a counselor in a big city about two hours away every other week for eighteen months. Every trip was like gaining new life and breath. My husband went to see this counselor one time, but later said that the counselor was "incompetent" and "off the wall." The counselor had the same credentials as my husband but apparently said some things that my husband did not want to hear. I finally was able to face myself honestly, to tell the truth about what I thought and felt, to talk about feelings, and finally begin to know that, like my children and every other human being, I was a person of value and worth. I finally realized that feelings were information; they were neither right nor wrong. I will never forget the words of a very trusted friend who came to see us during this terrible time. He said, "She has been hit by an eighteen-wheel truck, and you just have to let her go."

There is much more that could be said about this terrible time in my life, but I have chosen not to point fingers and also to accept blame for my own contribution to the breakdown of this marriage. I longed to be a whole person, and this journey was my own. Believe me, it was long and hard, this journey to wholeness, but a journey for which I am grateful today. After three years of separation, I knew that I was healthier apart from the relationship, but I had very strong feelings about divorce. When I finally realized that it was inevitable, my husband had already filed for divorce. I certainly didn't blame him.

It is with great joy that I can say today that my family is alive and well. When we all gather on special occasions, it is without tension and is a happy time. Our children know they are loved, and their children know how very much their grandpa and grandma love them as well. To God be the glory! Time is a healer, as well as the grace of God, and God is just waiting to offer this same healing power to you if you are struggling and want to be free.

# The Pickpocket:
# Marshmallows and Chocolate

Earlier in the book, I talked about the awesome wonder of creation and the imagery of the stones on the beach—some rough and some smooth, all washed by the ebb and flow of the tide. I talked about the stones being all lined up in a single row and how God spoke to me through them. I said that God often speaks to me through nature, that as I run and let the wind of God kiss my face and touch my heart, God's presence and truth is revealed to me in powerful ways.

This morning, before I began my run on that same beach, I asked God to give me a message that would speak to the content of this chapter. I invite you to come on that run with me as I tell you what my Best Friend said to me today. Hopefully, it will help you understand the message of this chapter. I continue to be amazed at the faithfulness of God to hear my heart and respond to me in ways that I can understand. Each of us hears differently, and God knows that. I think that is why God is ever-present, tuned into the hearts of God's people, and communicating in ways that are uniquely personal, all so that we can better understand God's incredible love for us.

Today's message came through the stones again, only this time in a much different way. The message was powerful, loud, and clear. This time the stones were *not* all lined up in a row. As I started to run on the beach, there were no stones. I was running barefooted, and the sand was soft and safe under my tender feet. Then that familiar, safe environment changed. There had been strong winds for the last few weeks that caused the waves to break with a thick head of foam. In places on the beach the foam was very thick, covering the beach as the tide subsided. It covered the sand and the rocks. The foam was interesting and intriguing; I had never seen this before. I could not see the rocks underneath. I stepped on a very rough rock, and it sent a shooting pain through my foot. The message was very clear. What seemed so safe, and once was, caused me a lot of pain. It hit me out of nowhere, so unexpectedly. I knew it was time for me to put on my flip-flops or move to higher ground. It hurt a lot, and I did not want to do it again. God's word often speaks to God's children in parables, for those who have ears to hear and eyes to see. This message was like a parable.

Farther down the beach, the foam was gone, and I could see the rocks scattered here and there. I was able to continue running, but I needed to pay attention to avoid stepping on the stones. I knew the rocks could hurt me, but if I was careful, I could avoid hurting myself by watching where I was going—kind of like being "in the world, but not of it." My safe, peaceful environment had changed so unexpectedly in such a short time, and it became very important for me to be cautious to avoid getting hurt.

Then the stones were everywhere. I could no longer avoid them, and I knew I needed to go higher up on the sand. Because I had already stepped on one rough stone and knew the pain of the experience, I was not about to do it again. In our lives and because of our human nature, we don't always learn from the pain of one bad experience, and we repeat it again and again. By moving farther up on the beach, I was able to continue my run, still enjoy the beauty of the experience and the environment, and remain in awe of the handiwork of God in this beautiful setting.

This is a difficult chapter for me to write because it is unlike the previous chapters. The previous chapters are about history. They are about experiences and events over which I had little or no control. They involve pain related to circumstances. They also are about experiences for which I have offered forgiveness, been forgiven, and have experienced the healing power of God's love. This chapter is about my choices, sometimes wrong ones, the consequences of which I will live with all my life. It is about compromise and settling for less than what God intended for my life. I will be forever grateful for the healing forgiveness of God and God's mercy. However, unfortunately, we humans are not so generous with our love and forgiveness. When we make wrong choices, hurt is usually involved. We either hurt ourselves or others, and often both. We hurt the people we love, and once the wound has been inflicted, it often takes a long time to heal. Unfortunately for some, the wound is never completely healed. It is only by the personal, loving work of The Healer in our lives that we are able to truly forgive and experience total healing and freedom.

Let me tell you about a sermon I heard recently. The pastor asked who in this very large congregation liked chocolate. Of course, many people raised their hands. He then stepped down from the pulpit and approached a woman whose hand was raised. He asked her if she liked chocolate, if she liked it a lot. She said yes. He then unwrapped part of a very large chocolate bar and told her to smell it. It smelled wonderful. He told her to lick it, and she did. It was delicious. She wanted more; she wanted to eat the whole thing. Then he told her to put the chocolate in her lap and not touch it, lick it, or smell it again. How could she keep from smelling it? It was right there in front of her! That seemed just about impossible to a hardcore chocolate lover. The pastor then went back into the pulpit and started throwing marshmallows out into the congregation. He had lots of marshmallows, and the people were all excited, eager to reach out and catch one. They seemed so harmless, so sweet, so tasty, so much fun. Then he said, "We are *all* only one marshmallow away from destruction!" That was totally unexpected. All of a sudden those soft, fluffy sweet morsels didn't taste the same. The message: Know the marshmallows in your life. Do you know yours?

I knew that I had been making choices that were not pleasing to God. My love for God was very real, but I had rationalized my behavior too many times, and I was living with much inner turmoil. I knew that I loved God and said that God was the most important person in my life but I was making choices that were not pleasing to God. All the while I was focusing on the fact that God was a God of mercy and grace, ignoring that I was not being accountable for my behavior. As long as I could say I did not do such and such, I could justify what I was doing.

After several months of struggling, I made an appointment with my pastor to talk about my struggles. I was tired of the turmoil in my soul. I tried to tell myself that I was happy, but I knew that I was not. I was experiencing some health problems, and the doctor told me that if something didn't change, my health problems would compound. I didn't want that to happen, and I was tired of living with the conflict in my soul. I wanted to once again experience the peace and safety that comes with knowing my life was in tune with God's heart.

I went to see my pastor. He knew that faith was important and personal to me. He recognized my turmoil and listened carefully. Then, with much wisdom, he said to me, "Satan has just about picked your pocket clean. I am glad you are here. There is hope."

You guessed it, the pickpocket is Satan himself. The marshmallows and chocolate are those temptations in our lives that trip us up, make us vulnerable, and lure us into situations that sometimes impact our lives with eternal consequences. Often they are disguised. They look beautiful and irresistible, and appear to be too good to be true. If we are not really in tune with our inner being and are not totally honest with ourselves, we can be blinded to the ways of the pickpocket. Did you know that in the beginning Lucifer was an angel who lived in heaven with God, but then wanted more power to be equal with God and was thrown out of heaven? He is wise and devious, and he knows where we are weak and where we have unmet needs. Satan doesn't mess much with those who consistently make choices and decisions familiar to his camp, those who give God little or no place in their lives. He already has them in the palm of his hand. Where he works overtime and ever so subtly is with those believers who are hurting, who are visibly in turmoil, who struggle with pain and injustice, whose lives are out of order. Satan loves to prey on those who are vulnerable, those who feel unloved, unappreciated, abused, and alone. Beware of the pickpocket who is always on the prowl!

Everyone's marshmallows are different. What one believer struggles with may be foreign to another believer. That is often why some believers seem to be so intolerant of the mistakes of others. Be not deceived—all believers are the target of the pickpocket. *No one* is exempt. It is critical that you recognize the marshmallows in your life and protect yourself against their destructive impact upon you when you give in to them.

I am grateful today that now I am no longer afraid to call my marshmallows by name and talk to God about them. For far too long I was unable to be honest with myself and was unable to recognize the marshmallows in my own life. Consequently, I would make repeated wrong turns and not understand why. I would even say to myself, *How could I have done that?* I now understand that it is better to be honest, to know myself, and to recognize my marshmallows when they present themselves.

Please understand that marshmallows or chocolate may not be bad in or of themselves, but if they present themselves to you at a time when you are feeling personally weak or troubled, they can knock you off your feet and cause you to lose your balance.

It's like the stones on the beach. When they were covered with foam, I did not see them until I stepped on one. When the stones became more plentiful, I needed to be very careful to avoid them, to pay attention to where I stepped in order to protect myself.

This is more like the reality of life. There are stones and marshmallows all around us, but as we focus on our path and recognize them, we can continue successfully on our way without being affected by the potential danger. We need to keep our focus on the loving care of God to meet our every need, resting in and claiming God's protection from all that is personally destructive. God knows our hearts and wants good things for each one of His children. However, when the stones and marshmallows fill the path and there is no safe place to run, it is time to go higher on the beach and turn away from that which is destructive to find a safer place to avoid harm. It requires deliberate action. We tend to recognize blatant ungodliness or clearly evil environments or situations. More times than not we can stay away from them.

Many years ago when I was in a difficult situation after I had made a wrong choice, I remember saying to my husband, "I don't belong here." Have you ever been in that situation? Did you wonder how it happened?

It is far more difficult to recognize the subtle presence of Satan in our circumstances than it is to recognize the blatant presence of evil. That is why it is so critical that you recognize the marshmallows in your life, call them by name, and never think that you are immune to their destructive power. If you want to be truly free, treat yourself to this gift of recognition and allow God to speak to you and set you free.

Remember, marshmallows and chocolate are temptations. It is only when we succumb to their power that they become sin. Don't be afraid to identify the marshmallows in your life and talk to God about them. God loves you so much and wants you to be safe and free. After all, God is your savior, your protector, and the one who loved you enough to die for you.

# Fairy Tale Turned Nightmare

I had been separated for about a year. I was working hard at dealing honestly with my life and wanting to be the best mom I could be. I was finally beginning to be able to identify some positive qualities in myself and actually starting to like myself for who I was. I had insights and opinions. I was a good listener, and people confided in me. I was beginning to have a positive approach to life and saw each new day as an opportunity to grow and to become. I continued to search the scriptures for life-giving treasures that spoke to my heart.

And I had a new appreciation for those who did not judge because I had experienced some very judgmental church people who I felt had written me off because of the separation. I have heard it said before that "the church is the only institution on earth that shoots its wounded." I experienced some of that wounding. However, I have been amazed how much understanding and acceptance can come from others who have been wounded themselves. They are not nearly so quick to judge. My faith and dependence upon God continued to grow in spite of the occasional darts that came my way. I was on the road to wholeness, and it felt good.

During the years of my marriage, I felt like my relationship with my birth family was fragile, to say the least, and my life was divided into two parts: before marriage and after marriage. Because I had not yet dealt well with the lack of emotion expressed by my mother and my inability to understand why she had not protected me, my relationship with her was strained. My stepfather had long since apologized for his rejection of me by saying that he realized that my mother was 90 percent of the problem and not me), and I was working at establishing a better relationship with him. But because of the underlying family dynamics and my inability to see my mother for who she really was, it was just easier to live my life in another part of the country in the church family, where people were valued and Christian values were a way of life. My mother was a very faithful church member, but I never recognized the presence of Christian values and faith lived out in our home.

As I think about it now, I wish my social worker husband had helped me recognize the good qualities in my upbringing. He didn't much like being in my family home either, so it was easy to stay away. But we all know that where we come from, and our family systems are an integral part of who we are, like it or not. He and I stayed away so much that we were only home for Christmas one time in twenty-two years, and we only took our family there one other time in all those years.

Critical to the healing process in these middle years of my life was the uniting of my current life with my former life, my roots and evolvement into adulthood. It all started with an invitation to my twenty-fifth class reunion. I had never been to a class reunion and was excited about seeing old friends. I looked forward to reminiscing about our winning softball and basketball teams in elementary school and junior high, our great YMCA camp experiences, our positive high school memories, and those long conversations about what was important in life and what we looked forward to. I had sent in my reservation to the reunion committee, and in a matter of weeks, I would reconnect with old friends and experiences.

Let me tell you about the fairy tale. Think about the definition of a fairy tale. *Merriam-Webster* says that a fairy tale is "marked by seemingly unreal beauty, perfection, luck, or happiness." When I think of a fairy tale, I think make-believe, too good to be true, pretend, perfect, romantic, enchanting, and "they lived happily ever after." Hold onto these thoughts.

On several occasions through the years Mr. First Love had called when he was in the area and wanted to come and visit. I always told him that I did not think that was a good idea. We had each made our own choices, and I did not think he would be coming to see my husband or my children, so his visiting would not be right. I encouraged him to be a good husband and father and said goodbye.

The phone rang. Imagine my surprise when it was the voice of Mr. First Love on the other end. Now the situation had changed and I was much more vulnerable. He had seen my name among the list of persons who had made reservations for the reunion, and he wanted to see me. He said that he had not had any relationship with his wife for more than five years. I talked to my counselor about this. The counselor encouraged me to go to the reunion, to not be afraid to see him, to have a good time, and to enjoy the opportunity to reconnect with my past. The counselor said a dinner out wasn't going to hurt anyone.

It was a wonderful reunion. People greeted me with warmth and affection. I was feeling free and happy with myself. I realized that a part of me would always be in the land of my roots, that a blending of both worlds was who I was. Amazingly, the two worlds could actually live together. What a revelation! It was not a matter of one being right and the other being wrong.

Mr. First Love was the first to greet me. He treated me like a queen, like I was the most beautiful woman in the world. This was not exactly how I recalled my relationship with him some thirty years before. He was so attentive and thoughtful. We talked, and I shared with him that I had found a safe place in my personal relationship with God. My life was focused in that hope and reality. I was grateful for three wonderful children, and life was getting better all the time. I shared that I was grateful for a life of meaning and value, and he seemed to want to hear about that life and how I came to experience it.

The reunion was a three-day event, and although I interacted with others throughout the event, Mr. First Love was at my side most of the time. It is hard to remember the specific events of the weekend, but I do remember that I left thinking that he really did care about me, that maybe he was different and his life had purpose. It was a good thought, one I wanted so much to believe. I returned home, back to my separate world, feeling refreshed and reconnected with people who had been such an integral part of my early life. Even today I look forward to every opportunity to reconnect with these friends.

As you might have guessed, my contact with Mr. First Love did not end with the reunion. We talked on the phone frequently. Before long he told me that he was moving into a house with a friend in his neighborhood, and he was filing for divorce. His mother had told me that his marriage was a mistake from the beginning. Apparently it was a big wedding with a reception at the country club, and status was important. He had said that his wife had "tricked" him into having children, and that his wife, his mother-in-law, and his single sister-in-law were an inseparable threesome. They, along with his two daughters, had their lives, and he had his life and his work. When I had encouraged him to be a good husband and father, I remember him saying, "What do I know about being a good father?" I thought that was kind of a strange response, but I didn't really press him on it at the time. I should have.

He continued to call me, sometimes several times a day. He wanted to see me. He wanted me to go back for a visit. He wanted to come and see me. Then he started sending me cards—endearing cards, funny cards. It seemed like a card every day. I must admit it felt good to be desirable, to be wanted. We reminisced about the things that were fun in our past. We even returned to the taquito stand where we had found ourselves after the motorcycle races some thirty-plus years before. Why did I encourage the relationship to grow? After all the hours of counseling and soul searching, how could I have been so enlightened and yet so blind? There were probably a number of reasons.

He told me over and over how much he loved me, how much he wanted to be with me. He told me I was beautiful. He called me princess. He showered me with gifts, something he had never done before. Remember the token perfume gift that Marg had given him to pass on to me, the one her students had given her that she did not want? He couldn't buy me enough things. What a contrast this was to my experience of having no allowance and negative numbers in the checkbook.

Surely he must be different. He no longer smoked, and he spoke much more freely now. I did notice that he was much more opinionated than I had ever known him to be. I guess I thought that was good, since before he had never expressed any feeling or emotion. He felt strongly about things now, and he was motivated, something else that I had never seen in him before.

And yes, there was chemistry, something that had not been present in my life nearly all of my adult years. He treated me with kindness and respect for three years, so surely he was a different person from the young man I had known whose heart had grown lonely in Japan. It seemed like he must have outgrown the beer drinking stage and, most important to me, he seemed interested in learning about Christianity as a way of life.

On one visit he asked me to share more with him about my faith. We took a Bible and sat along the river in a park. He asked me questions, and I shared my personal experience and what had brought me to a place of peace in my own personal relationship with God. He had grown up in the church, and his father was an elder, but he said he had never known anyone who actually lived Christianity as a way of life. I had told him that it was very important to me and that I could not marry someone who was not a Christian. He asked me to show him passages that spoke of committing one's life to Christ and asked me to pray with him. At that time he said he wanted to make a commitment to a life of faith.

I really do think he was sincere. This was a major turning point in our relationship. There were many things to work out—far more than I had any idea—but I thought maybe it could work. He seemed so different. He seemed to be responsible, had a good job, liked to travel, and wanted me again to be a part of his life. He wanted to show me things I had never seen, give me opportunities to experience things I had never experienced. He would ask me about something, and I would say, "I have never done that," or "I don't know anything about that." He would always say, "But you would like to, wouldn't you?" In some ways it was like he thought I had been deprived all of my adult life and now he was going to make it up to me.

Thus the fairy tale began, the one that was supposed to end with "and they lived happily ever after."

We were married the day after New Year's in our hometown. It was a very small wedding with just a few family members and some very close friends. We both wrote our own vows focused on the importance of God going before us and being the center of our relationship together.

It was an exciting, happy time, and there was lots of reminiscing about our life as kids. There was comfort in the fact that we knew each other's families and we had grown up with similar backgrounds and family values. Those family values have a far different meaning for me today than they did fifty years ago.

We had a delightful reception at a lovely restaurant in a seaport village. The meal and interaction with special friends is a wonderful memory. Much to my surprise, he had even brought high school graduation pictures of us to the reception. I was amazed that he had kept them throughout the years.

Later that week I returned home and he remained in our hometown. I had to be on his pension plan for a year before he retired, so we agreed that he would finish up his twenty years with his employer and then retire. Besides, I thought it would be good for him to remain in the area with his girls, especially during their high school years. It all made sense, except the part about the girls. I knew that their relationship with him was strained, but little did I know how much or why. It was not until a few years later that I realized the depth of his girls' resentment toward him.

I loved to travel. He loved to travel. However, he wanted to travel with no fuss and no mess—definitely no camping! I loved the outdoors. I loved to hike, to camp, to walk, and to enjoy nature. He liked all of it but from a different perspective—from an armchair. He had absolutely no interest in exercise.

He had told me I did not need to ask for anything and that I could buy what I wanted. It was such a change for me, since most of my adult life I had had little or no access to money for anything but necessities. This seemed so strange to him, and he wanted me to have nice things. He wanted me to look nice. He wanted me to have nice jewelry. He wanted to be seen with me.

And he was very affectionate. Affection was something I craved. I wish I could tell you that I was affectionate too, but I think I was not. I was starved for affection but found it difficult to give it in return. He would hold my hand or put his arm around me in public, and I loved it. It felt so wonderful to feel wanted. So much so that I think even from the beginning, I failed to recognize red flags when they popped up, probably because I was so needy. My need for affection seemed to overpower everything else, especially anything negative.

We did have many enjoyable times together. We traveled to places I had never seen. When we stayed in hotels, he would call ahead and have flowers waiting for us in the room upon our arrival. On one occasion on a cruise, he had roses waiting for us in our cabin. He was a romantic, and I loved that part of him. This was something I had never experienced with him in our relationship as kids. One time when I went to the hairdresser for a haircut, a bouquet of balloons was waiting for me. The hairdresser thought that was incredibly thoughtful. It was only later, after he told me that he knew where I was every minute of the day, that I first began to recognize his obsessive/compulsive behavior.

We were married the day after New Year's. We spent a few days in a lovely beach city, and then I returned home to my children. We planned a delayed honeymoon trip to Hawaii in April. In the months between, he was able to visit every four to six weeks, and his coming was filled with excitement. It was something to look forward to.

I had never been to Hawaii and was excited about the upcoming trip. We had planned for several days in Maui and several days in Kauai. Hawaii was beautiful. We attended an Easter service on the lawn of the hotel overlooking the area where the whales were migrating, and the weather was perfect. He liked to shop, and I soon learned of his favorite things to look for on shopping trips: T-shirts, luggage, and Hawaiian shirts. He was into matching outfits, but I was not. He seemed to accept this without any ado. His interests were really quite different from mine.

The nightmare begins here. We went to visit a hotel on the northern coast of Kauai. Some friends were giving a week's stay at this resort to the daughter of their friends as a honeymoon gift. They wanted us to check it out for them. That seemed harmless enough and an opportunity to see more of the island. We were both game to go. It was a beautiful place. But oh, was I in for a shock! This was the first of many such experiences that I would encounter in the years to come. It was after this experience that his own words, "I can get ugly in a heartbeat," became reality for me.

Little did we know that this was a timeshare resort. Little did I know that he did not like surprises. (There was much that I was about to learn about him.) When the person who was showing us the property explained that it was a timeshare property, the rage began. I had learned over the years to be polite in public no matter what and to not make a scene about anything. This was especially ingrained in me by my former husband, and rightly so. To me this was the scene of all scenes. He lashed out at the salesperson who was taking us on the tour in front of all the other people in the lobby. I can't remember all he said, but his anger and rage were full-blown. I don't know how long the actual encounter took, but I do know that I could not get out of there fast enough. It seemed like an eternity. I was shocked, humiliated, and incredibly embarrassed. How could this be? Where was the kind and thoughtful man I had just married?

I tried to discuss what had happened with him, but he was adamant that he had been tricked, and no one was going to do that to him! The ride to the other end of the island was painful. I cried and he drove. At one point he stopped the car, opened the trunk, threw a Kleenex box at me without saying a word, and started back on the road. When we got back to our hotel, I sat on the balcony sobbing. In my head I kept saying to myself, *What in the world have I gotten myself into?* I don't really remember how that incident was resolved, but you can be sure it was never forgotten. I don't know what we did next, but I tried to push the incident out of my mind. You know, pretend it did not happen.

There was another incident in Maui a few days before that. He wanted to buy a card to send back to his friends at work. Marriage was a very serious thing to me, not something to be taken lightly or joked about, and modesty and sexual expression were a very private matter. I was mortified when he was trying to decide which card with half-naked women he wanted to send to his friends. The thought of it seemed so disrespectful to me, making light of something I took so seriously, so personally. I was probably much too sensitive and he much too insensitive, but the tears flowed nevertheless. I was humiliated and found it hard to understand how he could do that to me. He could not understand why I thought it was such a big deal. I think this was the beginning of his resentment toward me for anything that smacked of what he called "Goody-Two-shoes."

We returned to the mainland and told everyone that it was a wonderful trip. Then I traveled back home.

I had not told my children that I had gotten married until just before the trip to Hawaii. I know that may seem strange, but I didn't want to do anything that would disrupt their school year, especially that of my son who was a senior in high school. He was a star basketball player hoping for a college scholarship, and I did not want to do anything that would jeopardize his basketball career, especially if it involved an emotional adjustment. I knew that my new husband was not going to come to live with me until after he retired, so there was plenty of time for my kids to get used to the idea before he actually came to stay. One night around the dinner table, they said something about me "getting a life," so I finally said to them, "Remember, you told me I should get a life? Well, I did." They were shocked. They seemed excited, and it seemed like a happy moment.

In the months between our marriage and our first anniversary, he and I talked daily. I tried to encourage him to maintain regular contact with his daughters to show interest in their activities and to work at strengthening his relationship with them. I encouraged him also to work at re-establishing a more positive relationship with his father, Jack, who lived only a few blocks away from him.

Jack was thrilled about our marriage, and he and his wife welcomed me with open arms. Jack said that I was "the best thing that ever happened to the family." It seemed like some of the bitterness my husband had experienced in his teen and early adult years was waning, and he was recognizing the importance of family in a new way. I was encouraged.

We spent our first anniversary on a beautiful island in the Puget Sound off the coast of Seattle and then took a ferry to Victoria, British Columbia. It was a delightful trip. We also spent a few days with his mother, Marg. She was most affirming of me but clearly expressed comments of displeasure or irritation with her son. It seemed so cruel to me. It appeared she did not like him because he was so very much like his father, whom she despised. I felt badly for him when she would make negative comments directed toward him. I am sure he felt that no matter what he did, he could never please either one of his parents. Unfortunately, that is exactly how his own children felt about him. I was beginning to understand why he chose to keep a distance from his family.

When we returned from our anniversary celebration, we went our different ways. It was in the following week that he decided he was going to retire, to leave everything he had ever known and come to be with me. His decision came out of the blue; we had not discussed it when we were together. I had really tried to encourage him to stay where he was and work at his relationship with his daughters. I also knew it would be a big adjustment for him to leave everything he had ever known. It would be a new environment with new people and a life with my three children, who were very different from his own. Everything would be new. He had not been involved in the lives of active teenagers. The way my children had been raised was very different from the way he had raised his own children, and I was concerned about the adjustment for everyone. I was very actively involved in the lives of my children and was concerned about all aspects of their development. I was committed to their support in every area—physical, spiritual, social, emotional, etc.

It was not long before I discovered that his definition of parenting was completely different from mine. To him, parental support meant providing food and shelter for kids until they were eighteen, looking good from the outside, and being absolved of any responsibility thereafter. Because he left home when he was nineteen and he had little positive interaction with his family, I think he thought that was the way it was supposed to be. He did not see any need for extended family interaction and had little sense of the importance of family relationships. Although red flags about such things had popped up from time to time in our discussions, I guess I chose to ignore them because of all the personal attention he showed me. In the years ahead, many of the disagreements or violent outbursts had to do with family and relationships.

It was only after we were married and he had come to live with me that I realized that he was like Jekyll and Hyde, sometimes nice, sometimes not nice. He had strong negative feelings about adoption. And I had three adopted children! He simply could not understand how anyone could love anyone else's children or, for that matter, why they would even want to. What a terrible shock this was to me. His parents had little appreciation for adoption as well, although I think they had a certain respect for me even though they couldn't understand it. This kind of thinking was so foreign to me. I saw my children as beautiful gifts from God, and I loved each of them with every part of my being. I remember the first major disagreement occurred only a month or so after he had come to stay. It was my first introduction to his foul mouth and his sick understanding of what it meant to be a parent. I was devastated.

And then there was the matter of mistakes. Mistakes were avoidable; no one was permitted to make a mistake. Accidents were not permissible. If a person was smart, they would not make mistakes. If you forgot something, you were irresponsible. He even expressed resentment when my mother left a jacket at the house. There was only one way to do things correctly—his way. If you planned carefully, you could avoid all surprises. He did not like surprises because if there was a surprise, then he was not in control.

It did not take me long to realize how very inflexible he was. He was not open to new ways of doing things or new ideas. He had set ideas about the value of things and the value of people (he thought some were more valuable than others), and he was big on stereotypes. Although he said he wanted to know more about Christianity as a way of life, he had no understanding of the equality of all humankind in the eyes of God or the value of every created being. He had no concept of mercy and forgiveness, and no understanding of the need for a Savior. He was self-sufficient and in control. He even criticized me for the way I flushed the toilet or how I put down the lid. He could be in another part of the house and tell me that I was going to break the lid because of the way I put it down. It's pretty bad when you can't even go to the bathroom in peace. If I ever drove through a puddle, I was irresponsible, and if I scraped the tire against the curb, it was a major offense.

As you can imagine, there were plenty of opportunities for disagreement, and I was finally learning to stand up for what I believed. The more I stood firm on matters that were counter to what he believed, the more potential there was for his outbursts of anger. I don't think he had ever had anyone stand up to him before, especially not a woman, and he definitely resented it.

He often criticized me for my Christian values and would say hurtful, hateful things. I would tell him that there were only two things that would make me angry: disrespect and injustice. I further told him that when he treated me with disrespect, I would walk away from him and remove myself from his presence so that he could not physically hurt me. There were occasions when he became so angry and lashed out at me that I was afraid of him. He would always say that it was my fault because I had "pushed his buttons."

It sounds really terrible, but he always held it against me that on one occasion I bit him. What you need to know is that I bit him because he had me in a headlock and that was the only way I could get away from him. Another time he was spewing out venom about something that was important to me and pounding his finger into my chest. I grabbed his finger to make him stop. He later referred to that incident as the time when I almost broke his finger, as if I were the violent one. Occasionally he would say that he was sorry and that he knew he could be very difficult to live with. That was an understatement.

Once early in our marriage, we were on vacation visiting his brother's family at a beach house. We had all gathered for dinner at a quaint little restaurant, and it seemed the family time was good. When we left the restaurant, he and I were discussing the dinner table conversation, and the subject turned to his father. I cannot remember exactly what was said, but I asked a question. He became enraged and started yelling at me. I asked him to stop the car and let me out, saying that I did not want to be in his presence when he was in that frame of mind. Finally I was able to get out of the car. It was dark, and I had no idea where I was or how to get back to the beach house. All I knew was that I would be safer away from him than with him. He took off at a high speed, spewing gravel all over me. I began to walk. I walked and I cried, alone in the dark, wondering how I had gotten myself into such a situation.

The nightmare was not always rooted in outbursts of anger or violent situations. Many times the pain came from his cruel response to an unanticipated situation. I will give you just a few examples. We were out for a pleasant bike ride. The path narrowed, and I decided to go off the path to exit the area because the posts defining the path were close together. I thought I could go off to the left and not need to slow down. Little did I know that there was a transparent nylon cord strung across that section of the grass. I was riding at a good pace and ran into the cord before I realized what was happening. The faster I went, the more the cord stretched tighter and tighter across my arm, deepening the rope burn that covered half of my arm. The burn was deep and very painful. When he saw that I had stopped, he came back to see what was wrong. He criticized me for being so stupid, as if to say it served me right for not paying attention. I was so humiliated that I forced back the tears, rode to a drinking fountain, ran cold water over the wound, and continued on with the bike ride. I later found out that this area had been roped off with yellow flags, but the flags had all blown to the side, making the roped-off area invisible. I am reminded of this incident every time I look at my arm, as I have a six-inch scar that looks like my arm was cut in half and put back together. I always hope that a suntan will cover it up, but it never happens.

On another occasion, Jack and his new wife came to visit, and I asked Jack a question about my car. He asked me if I had asked my husband about it, but I said that I had not because he was always so quick to blame me for anything that went wrong with the car. It just was not worth the anxiety to ask him certain questions. I went on to say that if anything ever happened to me or if I was in an accident, I would never call my husband because he would only make the situation worse. In a time of crisis, one needs to experience compassion and support, not criticism and condemnation. Jack was shocked at my response. He said that was a terrible way to live in a marriage and asked why I put up with that. I told him it had taken me twenty-five years to learn to be compassionate and caring and that someone believed in me, so I needed to offer that same opportunity to him. I still believe this was the right response, but I am not nearly so naïve now. I am far wiser today about taking care of myself and not allowing myself to be abused.

One of the most emotionally painful incidents occurred when I had major surgery about seven years into the marriage. I had not felt good for some time but had said very little to my husband about how I was feeling. By this time in the marriage, I pretty much kept everything I was thinking and feeling to myself. I had been under a physician's care for several months in hopes of avoiding major surgery, but it became inevitable. I came out of surgery to be told that I was diabetic, that my organs were not where the doctor thought they should be, and that my bladder had been cut in the process. I had a six-foot catheter and would need to have it for at least a month. Following surgery I experienced complications and was in the hospital twice as long as initially anticipated. My husband came to see me only a few times for a few minutes, saying that he did not like hospitals and did not feel comfortable there. I felt very much alone. On the day I was released, he insisted that I go from the hospital to the car repair place to pick up his car where the air conditioner was being replaced. I was very weak and not supposed to drive for about four weeks, but he insisted that I drive that day, that moment! Then the day after I went home, he told me that if I was going to be sick for six weeks, maybe I should go somewhere else. The pain of this rejection is still with me today. At the time that he left the marriage, he did tell me that he was sorry for his insensitivity. He knew that he had been very cruel.

Over the years there were many times when my husband's responses to women, even young girls, seemed inappropriate. He was very touchy-feely, and not everyone appreciated it. It was like he did not know what was appropriate and what was not. On one occasion, he invited a cheerleader friend of my son to our house for dinner. He invited her to come an hour or so before I got home from work, which was very inappropriate and made the girl feel very uncomfortable. The girl later told me how uncomfortable she was, and I asked him to apologize to her. He kept a picture of her under the glass on his desk. He finally did write a note of apology to the young woman when I tried to explain how he might feel about it had it been his own daughter, but I am not sure to this day that he thought he had been inappropriate in any way.

Another time he spent the day garage sale shopping with a young single mom he had met at work. She lived a few blocks away from us. I thought it was a nice gesture when he took the lawnmower over to her house to mow the grass, but that was before I knew that he had spent the day with her.

It always seemed he could interact better with women than he could with men. He had lots of male acquaintances, but no one knew him really well. He said that I was the only one who knew him well, maybe even better than he knew himself.

I don't know where or when the marriage actually fell apart or exactly how I contributed to the demise, but I do know that we both were increasingly unhappy. He became more and more negative. When I was offered a major promotion at work, he was not supportive and later told me that he resented that I took the job. He had a serious resentment toward administration, and by taking the job, I became part of administrative leadership.

I remember asking him on many occasions why he did not tell me about who he really was before we married. His answer was, "Because I knew you would not marry me if you knew." My response was always the same: "You are right, I would not have married you had I known." I felt like I needed to be honest. Maybe I should not have been quite so direct.

He told me that everything in life for him was a quest. I guess I was just one of those quests. That would explain the "I can get ugly in a heartbeat" comment. As long as he was on the quest, he could be kind, control his responses, and pursue the goal. When the goal was achieved, then he could let his true colors show. That's why I called him "Jekyll and Hyde." The scary part was not knowing which person was going to be revealed in a given situation.

I knew about his involvement with his girlfriend for approximately two years before he left the marriage. At first he gave subtle hints, and then his actions became increasingly more blatant. For example, he left a telephone message saying he was going to be gone for a few days to visit a friend in a city a few hours away saying that I needed to have some time alone. When he returned home, he had brought the box of leftover food from a very nice restaurant in a different city—where we had previously gone for a special night out—and put it in the refrigerator for me to see. I knew that he had spent the weekend with his girlfriend and taken her to the special place for dinner.

On another occasion he and his girlfriend talked about the "LBS" in my presence. The "LBS" was the "little black skirt" (size eighteen) that he had ordered for her on my computer at work. I received the confirmation of the order on my computer as well.

And then there was the time he had spent the weekend Christmas shopping with his girlfriend. I asked her husband if he was aware that she had gone shopping with my husband. He was shocked! He thought she had attended a spiritual retreat in Chicago. When I confronted the girlfriend, who was supposed to be my friend, she did not deny that she had been on the shopping trip, but she did deny her involvement with my husband. When she told him I had confronted her, he told me that he would make life very difficult for me and threatened to divorce me if I ever confronted her again.

Others had questioned their relationship as well, and apparently someone had sent an anonymous letter to her husband encouraging him to get his house in order. My husband then told me to "call off my dogs or it was going to get really ugly." He admitted that he never tried to hide anything. When I gave him a book to read entitled *Boundaries in Marriage*, I asked him to read one specific chapter. He read the chapter and then told me that the chapter was about him and that he was clearly aware of his actions. I asked him, "If you know there is hope for a different way and forgiveness is available, why wouldn't you take it?" His answer was simply, "Because it is too hard."

So you see, Jekyll was really Hyde, and that's why the fairy tale did not end happily ever after. Mr. Hyde said that I did nothing wrong in the marriage, but I guess I will always wonder. My husband left the marriage to go live with another man's wife. They finally married after living together for ten years.

I could tell you of many more incidents, but my point is not to make him look bad. The reality is that even though I had grown a lot in my understanding of myself, I was still blind to my need for affection and personal attention. I ignored the red flags and proceeded to make my choices based on unmet needs rather than a better way that God might have for me. I did not ask for God's opinion in the matter, which was very unfortunate.

I told my husband and his girlfriend that I did not blame either of them, that I was living with the consequences of my own wrong choices. Once again I had compromised part of my own body, mind, and spirit because of an unmet need in my life. Hopefully I will not make the same mistake again. I know that my life without him is better, but those feelings of failure crop up every now and then. I have gained so much compassion for others who have struggled and better understand how easy it is to make wrong choices. I am so grateful that God is not finished with me yet.

# Detours

Have you ever taken a detour? I'm sure you have. Some have taken many detours, others only a few. What are your first thoughts when you see a detour sign on the road? *What's this? What an inconvenience. I don't have time for this.* Sound familiar?

What is a detour? To me, a detour is a deviation from an original plan. I'm on the road to a destination, and all of a sudden there is a roadblock. I have to take another route. The purpose of a detour is to get me back on the road to my final destination. Sometimes it is for my protection. Other times it is just necessary. The goal is to get me where I need to go. How I get there is not what matters most, although we often see it as an intrusion on our precious time. So it is with the detours in our lives. Sometimes we make choices that take us far from the path that leads to peace and safety. I call these choices detours. Sometimes we make one wrong turn after another and we become lost, without a clue which direction we should go. We are never alone, but it sure feels like it.

Sometimes we know the right way to go, the most direct way, but we are adventurous. We think we can try a new way that could be more exciting. Before we know it, we are lost again. When we take our own detours off of the given path of God's perfect plan for our lives, we set ourselves up for pain. We compromise and settle for less than what is best for us. The consequences of our detours sometimes impact the rest of our lives in big ways. We must live with the consequences of our choices. But be of good cheer—God can use our detours to help us find our way back to God and to make us whole.

God weeps when we make wrong choices. But what God cares about most is that we are in close relationship with God, whether we have made God Lord and Savior of our lives, and whether we will spend eternity with God. We are all on a journey, and we all get on the road that leads to eternal life at different places. God cares not so much about where we have been but where we are going. God will always be with us; God will never forsake us. Even though we have made choices that are not pleasing to God, we are accepted where we are and invited to return to God. God offers a way of hope, a path that leads to good things. God can use the detours in our lives to bring us to wholeness.

Some detours are longer than others. How we respond to the detours in our lives has a tremendous impact on our future. Here is an example.

Many years ago my second husband and I were traveling cross-country in February. We had decided to travel the southern route in an effort to avoid possible snowfall farther north. About an hour east of Albuquerque, we came to a detour. If you are familiar with New Mexico, you know that there is a whole lot of nothing to the east and north of Albuquerque. There are mountains, and the area is very sparsely populated. You can drive for hours and not see anything but desert and sagebrush. It was five o'clock in the evening, and we had been driving all day. The sign just said "Detour." It didn't say how far or for how long. Little did we know that there had been a hazardous waste spill and the detour was more than a hundred miles. My husband was livid!

Because I was familiar with this part of the country, I knew that if we traveled north through the mountains, we could catch a highway that would take us across southern Kansas and eventually get us back on track. It was definitely not the scenic route—cattle feed lot after feed lot—but it was good road and would work for us without much inconvenience. I suggested this route to my husband, and he reluctantly agreed to trust me. This was a major deviation from the way we had planned to go. What if we ran into snow? What if we couldn't find anywhere to eat or sleep? My husband was hungry and tired from a long day of driving. He was in unknown territory, and he did not want to be there. He did not like surprises and was not very flexible, to say the least. Then, wouldn't you know it, it started to snow as the sun was going down. It was dark, we were beginning the climb into the mountains, and it was snowing! Needless to say, the tension was rising.

We made it through the mountains. Finally, at about nine o'clock at night, we came to a small town in northeastern Colorado. It was way past dinnertime, and there was only one place open where we could eat. This in itself was enough to make my husband an unhappy camper. We found an inexpensive motel where we spent the night. I was grateful we had found our way there safely without further inconvenience and that I was familiar with the southern route through Kansas. I felt like we had been protected and that God was going before us, meeting our every need. My husband, however, focused on being hungry and tired, and he was not feeling confident about where we were going next. We had experienced a detour, but the way we each responded to it was quite different. I was grateful and positive; he was negative, irritated, and skeptical. We have a choice about how we respond to the detours we take. We can become hardened and angry, or we can be grateful and hopeful.

The next morning we were able to get onto the main highway that took us across the southern part of Kansas. I have never seen or smelled so many feedlots in my life, but the road was good. We stopped to see a friend in Olathe and then there it was again—another detour. This time it was not for our protection; it was simply due to a lot of road construction. I do not even remember the details of what happened next, other than that there was a bus station close to the place where we finally decided to settle for the night. My husband was so out of sorts and so angry that it was just about impossible to be in the car with him. I was a fraction of an inch from leaving the motel, walking to the bus station down the street, and getting on a bus to go the rest of the way home.

There were a lot of emotional changes taking place in my husband's life right then, and I am sure that they played a big part in his inflexibility and his outbursts of anger. Knowing that did not make it any easier to live with him or to tolerate his behavior. He simply could not bend or adjust his thinking or his attitude to accept anything that was different from his plan. He hated surprises and anything he could not control. He was paralyzed by a situation over which he had no control, and his anger flared into a raging fire. His inflexibility affected everything he touched, everything he said, everyone in his path. The detour was not the problem; how he responded to it was. In this situation, his response was triggered by a much more significant personal issue: his need to be in control.

When we get off the main road and are traveling in unknown territory, we often find ourselves in difficult situations because we have unmet needs in our lives that have not been addressed. For example, the young woman who feels alone and unloved is often easy prey for the ego-centered young man who is out to use her, or anyone else, for his own self-pleasure. When the young woman realizes that she has been used, she feels more lonely, disappointed in herself, and guilty for her lack of discretion. This definitely affects the way she feels about herself, damaging her self-esteem. This is an example of a detour. Her behavior certainly was not in line with God's perfect plan for her, but it need not paralyze her from moving forward and getting back on the right path. If she is able to understand her own areas of weakness, forgive herself, and look to God for strength and forgiveness, she can be wiser and stronger in the future.

We are complex, needy human beings affected by the sin of Adam and Eve in the very beginning of creation. Most of us are not deliberately defiant or arrogant people who delight in making wrong choices. But we all have been wounded in one way or another and are sometimes controlled by the impact of that hurt on our lives. This causes us to make choices that we often regret. We are not always aware at the time that our choices are harmful until we discover that we cannot reverse their impact on our lives. Then we must live with the consequences of our behavior. There is no question that detours affect us. But God does not keep track of our detours. Rather, we are wooed to seek God with our whole being. If it takes one detour or many to get our attention, then so be it. Remember, it is our final destination that God is most interested in, and God promises to be with us every step of the way along the journey.

I have taken many detours in my life, and I am not proud of them. The detours have impacted my life in powerful ways. I think that forgiving myself has been even harder than accepting God's forgiveness. I look back and say, "How could I have been so stupid? Why was I so blind?"

I can't answer all of the questions. I do know that healing and growing and becoming is a process, a process that has taught me to better understand myself and offer hope to others. I hope the process has enabled me to help someone else avoid the same wrong choices. In spite of all the detours, or maybe because of them, I know that I would not be the person I am becoming today had it not been for all of the experiences I have encountered on this journey through life.

Think about your own detours. Has your self-esteem suffered because of your choices? Are you having trouble forgiving yourself? Do you feel like you have been scarred for life? If so, remember this: scars are reminders of wounds that have been healed. Look forward to what you are becoming, and don't focus on your shadow. If you want to truly be free and whole and full of life with meaning, then stay tuned for the chapter on gratitude about the wonder of God's love and forgiveness available to every child of God—available to you!

# Gratitude

As I write this chapter, once again I find myself reflecting on the awesome beauty of God's creation, this time on a pristine beach in the turquoise Caribbean. I am ending a week of writing with the hope of finishing the two remaining chapters of this book. When I am surrounded by such beauty, I often hear God speak to me in new and refreshing ways, powerful ways. This chapter was not included in my original book outline, but I have been overwhelmed by some of the symbolism I have experienced while here.

I rose early today to see the sunrise. It was a clear night, and the stars were brilliant. I listened quietly as the surf broke gently onto the sand—a soothing, almost melodious sound—again and again and again. I watched as the first glimmer of light graced the horizon. Next the clouds emerged. As the clouds rose, so did the light. The sky then burst into color—first pink, then orange, then bright blue. The dark sea turned from black to silver to blue. A huge orange sphere appeared on the horizon, first behind a cloud and then in all of its glory. A new day had dawned. I was reminded of the words from the song "Great Is Thy Faithfulness" that talk about God's mercies being new every morning. Indeed God's mercy is new every morning. I was reminded that I should think about this each day as I rise. I should ask to be shown God's mercy anew each day and know that God is faithful to provide for my every need.

I have just finished writing the chapter "Fairy Tale Turned Nightmare" and as you know, it did not have a very happy ending. I told the story not because I wanted people to feel sorry for me nor to make another person look bad. I told it because it was true, it was the real world, and I know that there are many wounded people who can identify with it. This story could have seemed very tame compared to the mental abuse and physical violence experienced by many women, violence so ugly that it is even too difficult to talk about, violence that has forever scarred the lives of countless women who were created beautifully in the image of God and then wounded by another wounded soul.

A tiny shell on the beach caught my eye. I picked it up and marveled at its transparency. Here it was on the beach among millions of shells, almost paper thin and still perfectly shaped. It seemed so fragile yet so perfect and unscathed. We are so much like that shell, so fragile yet so resilient. We do not have to develop an opaque shell, impenetrable by light. We can be transparent, allowing the light of God to shine in and out. We have been knocked down by the storms of this life, yet we do not stay down. We rebound, become stronger, and press on. We may be wounded, but we need not be destroyed. If we believe that God has a plan and a purpose for our lives, then we know that God can enable us to transcend any current situation. By the power of God's spirit within us, God enables us to soar like eagles above the storms of this life.

Just recently a friend sent me a thought for the day that said, "Life is not about waiting for the storm to pass; it is about learning how to dance in the rain." Another thought that came soon after that was, "Life is not what it is supposed to be; it is what it is." How we respond to it makes all the difference in the world. We can choose to be overpowered and overcome, or we can choose to grow, to forgive, and to rise above any situation or circumstance that imperils us.

I am reminded of the book I used to read to my children when they were very young, *Alexander and the Terrible, Horrible, No Good, Very Bad Day* by Judith Viorst. The story goes something like this:

> My ice cream cone fell on the ground,
> I fell and skinned my knee,
> And my best friend said she didn't want to be my best friend anymore.
> But then …
> I got a new ice cream cone,
> My knee got better,
> And my best friend changed her mind and decided I could still be her best friend.

Although this was a message in a children's book, the message is powerful and applicable to all of life. Let's face it, some days are better than others. Sometimes our lives feel like a roller coaster ride—one day up and the next day down. But there is good news: the joy that comes from an intimate relationship with a powerful loving God provides stability for us in troubled times. That intimate relationship becomes our safe haven, our peace, and our hope. That intimate relationship enables us to experience joy in the midst of any difficult situation. For many years I had a little saying on the bulletin board in my office that said, "Joy is in us, not in things." It is so true, and it comes from the Father of Life who loves us and knows our every need. God reaches out a hand and beckons us to take hold, to rest in God's care.

Our storms or crises may be different, but one thing is clear: if we refuse to get up or bounce back, our lives are in a sense paralyzed. If we refuse to forgive, we limit the healing that God has already provided for us. Forgiveness opens the door to peace and joy. When we stop blaming others and strive to become whole, God is merciful and meets us again and again, like God's mercies are new every morning, enabling us to become resilient like that very fragile seashell. Joy will take the place of anger and resentment, and peace will soothe our souls. We will indeed be grateful for all that is good, and the focus of our existence will be upon that which brings life and peace to us and others. Our wounds will be healed, and we will be free.

# The Love of My Life

It's never the same. Each time I come to the beach, I discover something new. I see the wonder of God's creation in a new way, from a new perspective. Some things are constant, like the rising of the sun and the breaking of the waves on the sand. But the impact of the breaking waves and the rising sun on the clouds and the horizon is always a beautiful mystery. This visit, the tide is high and the waves are big, crashing with a mighty roar as they kiss the earth, unlike anything I have ever seen here before. With each breaking wave comes a new impact, just as each new day begins with a mystery and ends with a different look. Indeed, the mercies of God are new every morning.

This literary journey began for me in this same setting several years ago. This visit brings me back to write the final chapters. It has been an interesting and exciting journey. It has been a journey of growth, a journey that has forced me to relive some very difficult and painful experiences in my life. However, throughout the journey I have been reminded of God's faithfulness, of God's forgiving love and mercy. God's voice, encouraging me to press on, has been clear whether I have been running on the beach, running in my neighborhood at sunrise, or simply quietly reflecting on God's peaceful presence in my life. There is so much for which I am thankful. As I reflect on my life, I can see how God has always protected and loved me. I can see that the experiences of my life have led me to become a whole person. I wish the same for you.

Recently I heard a sermon that illustrated this reality so well. A young girl was asking her mother what it meant in Romans 8:28 when it said, "All things work together for good for those who are called according to his purpose." The Living Bible says, "We know that all that happens to us is working for our good if we love God and are fitting into his plans."

This verse has been in my head since the death of my father. It was written on this hideous plaque with hot-pink flowers and lime-green leaves that was forever standing on the buffet in our eating area at home. It was given to my mother after the death of my father. Although my mother never talked about it, she always kept it in that spot. I think there were times when it brought comfort to her, but I also knew that there was something kind of holy about its presence in our home, even though I didn't understand why. I am so thankful now that I understand its meaning.

My mother probably would have described herself as a religious person, but personal faith was never talked about in our home. "Religious" probably meant that she went to church regularly, like all "good" people. My father rarely went to church with us, and my brothers definitely did not appear to be interested. The only time the Bible was mentioned was when my mother was so frustrated with my attitude or my behavior that she would tell me, "The Bible says ..." That was always so interesting to me, and irritating too, because I saw little evidence of what I will call the "Bible in action" in our home.

Please excuse my digression from the story I started to tell. The mother illustrated the Romans passage for her young daughter this way. She took a teaspoon of baking soda and asked her daughter to taste it. Can't you just about see the daughter's face when she put the baking soda on her tongue? Did it taste good? No. Was it awful? Yes. Then she proceeded to mix the baking soda and the other dry ingredients with the liquids, and she baked the cake. When the cake was baked, she asked her daughter to taste again. It was of course delicious. That is the way it is with life. We have all had "baking soda moments," but how we view them or what we do with them has everything to do with the way we view our life. When they are mixed together with all the ingredients in our life, they can produce something wonderful. We can either isolate those experiences and forever talk about how bad they were, or we can see them from a different perspective and know that God is in control, that "all things truly do work for good for those who love him and want to walk in his way."

I see each day of my life as a gift, as a choice. When someone asks me, "How are you?" I always think, *Fine, why not?* because every day I can choose whether I will go my way or choose God's way. Whether I have a good day or not is my choice. My heart and my head both know that God's ways are far superior to my own. I have not always chosen God's ways, but when the quality of my life (with God's way) has been so superior to life with my own choices, I often wonder why it sometimes seems hard to choose God's way.

I am so grateful for healing and wholeness in my life, and I want to encourage you, wherever you are on your journey, to reach out for that same hope and peace that calms the turbulent waters of our earthly existence. To that end, I invite you to walk with me now on my own personal faith journey. Your story may be different, but the same God of wonder, of healing, and of wholeness is there and waiting for anyone who comes with a sincere heart, just like the loving papa who opens his arms wide and invites the young child to crawl up into his lap to a place of comfort and safety.

This is one of the few happy childhood memories for me. I must have been somewhere between six and eight years old, when my maternal grandparents would pick me up and take me to their cabin for the weekend. We would go on Friday afternoon after school and come home on Sunday night. My brothers never went. I always felt loved by my grandparents, especially by my grandmother.

There was a little country church on the highway at the bottom of the hill of the winding country road that led to the cabin. Sometimes on Sunday mornings, I would walk down that winding road all by myself on my way to Sunday school at that little country church. (My grandparents were very active in their church at home, but they never went with me to the country church.) I don't remember anyone's name or any faces at that little country church, but I do remember that I felt loved at the cabin and on that country road, and I received some little gift every time I visited the church. They always seemed happy to see me. All I recall is that I felt peaceful there. I think this was one of my earliest memories of anything Godlike. I never talked to anyone about this. I guess it was just kind of like God introducing Himself to me for the first time. Anyway, I really liked the feeling and treasured it deep in my heart.

In my early elementary years, our family went to a big old Methodist church downtown. It was the same church my mother had attended as a young girl and teenager. We always went to Sunday school but never to "big church." I thought big church was for old people, and as I recall, there were lots of devices for the hearing impaired in the pews. (This might be why I thought it was only for old people.) Occasionally I would stay and go to big church with my grandparents, who were regular attendees. In the sanctuary there was a huge pipe organ and beautiful stained-glass windows. In my very young years, those things symbolized something Godlike for me. I do remember always having a tender heart toward things of God, although I really had very little understanding of Christianity (except for my experiences at Y Camp) until my personal faith encounter when I was twenty-two. It was then that I realized that Christianity was a way of life, not just a Sunday morning "must do to be good" event.

What was Christianity to our family? My parents' peers were their fellow Sunday school class members, and their teacher was a retired doctor whom they respected. For my brothers, it seemed the best thing about the church for them was the gym that was so typical of most old, large Methodist churches. Although there may have been consistent Biblical teaching along the way, it certainly is not what left an impression on me in those early years. Going to church for our family seemed like a social experience, at least for our parents. I cannot speak for my brothers. I do not remember any family discussion about the application of Biblical principles learned. Certainly it never occurred to me at that young age that Christianity was a way of life. When I was in first and second grade, my next older brother and I walked a few miles each way for Bible school in the summer. Bible school is a pleasant memory for me.

When I was in the third grade, our family moved away from the downtown church into a new subdivision with a different church, as did many of the families of my parents' peers. Thus ended the social experience for my parents, the activities in the gym for my brothers, and the big church experiences with my grandparents. Of course the new church had an organ (but not the big pipe organ) and stained-glass windows so representative of Methodist churches, but it was not the same. My father seldom went to church with us, and my brothers only went when they were forced to on special occasions, such as Easter and Christmas Eve. My best memory of this church was Christmas Eve services, which were always meaningful to me.

Like all good Methodist kids, I was encouraged to join the confirmation class when I was thirteen. In that era, Methodist children were baptized as infants and then confirmed as a group when they were thirteen. This might have been a meaningful entry into a life of personal faith for some, but I am sorry to say that the most memorable part of my confirmation experience was a field trip to a big observatory and zoo in the neighboring city. Nonetheless, deep in my heart was that same growing seed of spiritual consciousness that sustains me and gives me hope today. Even when I did not know God or recognize God's presence, God was with me, patiently waiting for me to come and sit in His lap.

I mentioned in an earlier chapter that the most significant spiritual experiences in my junior high and high school years were related to my participation in YMCA clubs and camps. It was during these Y experiences that I was becoming increasingly aware of the reality of a living and personal God. In my quiet moments alone, I would find myself talking to God. When I could not talk to my mother or it seemed she never cared or asked about what I felt, I would turn to God. Somehow I always knew that God would listen and that God really did care about me. I could pour out my heart to God and not be criticized. I always found comfort in my conversations with God. My personal friendship with God started way back then and remains the most meaningful relationship in my life today. God is so good and oh, so patient. During those "Hormones, Rough Road, and Confusion" years, it was my quiet one-on-one conversations with God that sustained me.

At that time I knew very little about the meaning of a personal faith commitment or discipleship, but I did know that God was real. I continued to go to church with my mother, but I had this growing resistance to institutional church and the need to get dressed up and make a good impression. Since the death of my father, I had become aware that the pastor prayed for those who mourned, but I remember little other than that. There were quotes from books and the ever-present singing of "Holy, Holy, Holy" and the doxology. It was not until I was twenty-one that I recall ever hearing a message of salvation. Please understand, the message may have been there; it may be that I just did not hear it. How could it be that I had all those years of church experience and no recollection of the message of salvation?

When Mr. Social Worker came into my life, he told me that all of the things I expressed as desires for my life were characteristic of Christian life and discipleship, but I had just never heard the message. His spiritual experience and maturity were a gift to me, opening a whole new way of life for me. For this I will be forever grateful.

My next significant spiritual experience came in the first year of my marriage when I found myself alone one night in that far away land with no friends. I turned on the TV and what should appear but a Billy

Graham crusade. Go figure—the essence of the American "God and country" message got through to a hippie nonconformist mentality! Something was happening inside of me. I remember tears streaming down my cheeks as they sang "Just as I Am." There was no question that God was speaking to my heart.

While I was battling with the temper tantrums that erupted from what I perceived to be my husband's attempts to control my life and destroy me spirit, I asked my husband one night to take me to his home church to pray. I remember it was dark and he went to the pastor's house for the key, then I went into the church all by myself. You see, at that time, I still associated the presence of God with a physical place. I had much to learn about God's presence in every situation, in every experience and that the Spirit of God was present within me wherever I found myself.

I was baptized as an adult, and I shared with the congregation then that I realized for the first time that Christianity was a way of life. This marked the formal beginning of a long but exciting journey for me.

I began to learn more and more about the teachings of Jesus and their implications for everyday life. I began to understand that Jesus's number one message was one of unconditional love for all, not "I will love you only if." Little by little I was beginning to understand the meaning of the verse that says, "Perfect love casts out all fear." I had been so fearful—of rejection, of failure, of not meeting expectations, whether they were the expectations of others or self-imposed. How could perfect love cast out all fear? Today I am still learning about these truths, but I no longer live in fear.

Three years into our marriage, my husband felt led to go to seminary in preparation for his calling to become a pastor. You might ask if I was afraid of this next step, of the implications associated with being a pastor's wife. Surprisingly enough, this was not one of my fears. By this time I was experiencing a growing desire to learn more and more about the teachings of Jesus and what it meant to appropriate God's power in my life. It was now easy for me to "talk the Christian language," even though I had not yet come to a place of total surrender so that I could truly know the power of God's spirit at work in me to direct my life. I wanted to be a good, supportive wife, and I was grateful for the positive changes that had taken place in my life.

Prior to moving to a new city for my husband's first year of seminary, our very close friends invited us to join their extended family for a week's vacation in Minnesota and Canada. It was on this trip that one of the persons traveling with us asked me question after question about the work of the Spirit of God in a Christian's life. She stated that she was ready to become totally surrendered to God and asked if I would pray for her to that end. What was I going to do? Like I said, I could talk the talk, but could not speak of total surrender because I had not come to that point in my own life. Finally, I said that I did not think that I could be helpful to her, but I was sure that her brother-in-law could. She asked if I would go with her. I said I would be happy to. Her heart was so sincere, and I knew that she was looking for a deep and meaningful spiritual experience in her life. She wanted to experience the power of God's presence in her like never before. I had that same desire but had not yet taken the step or had the courage to reach out and pursue it. I guess I was still afraid of what it meant to be totally surrendered to the Spirit of God.

We went to her brother-in-law and she told him of her desire to be "totally surrendered." I remember saying, "Oh, by the way, you can pray for me too." It was at that moment that the impact of my Christian experience became branded on my heart. Thus began the transforming power of God in my heart. It was the point at which my heart became alive to the teachings of Jesus, the point at which I began to learn about having "eyes to see" and "ears to hear." It was the beginning of the illumination of an incredible relationship with my very best friend in the whole world.

Please remember, I have said it was the *beginning* of a journey, not the arrival at a destination. In the years that have followed, the journey has taken me on a winding road up some very steep hills. There have been mountaintop experiences and very difficult times deep in the valley. However, there is no question about it, my life was transformed for the better that day when I finally said, "You can pray for me too." Since that day I have known without question that God's love is real, that God's presence within me is empowering, and that *nothing or no one* can take that away from me. Everyone has to come to God in their own way via their own route in their own time, but I believe every human being has the same desire to be loved unconditionally, to be empowered to make good choices, and to live at peace with themselves and with others. This is the gift of God to all who seek Him!

The year that followed was one of the most memorable and peaceful years in my life. My heart was pure, and I spent hours and hours studying the incredible life of Jesus and his impact on the lives of all he encountered. I had a deep desire to grow and pattern my life after the teachings of Jesus. Having been an impressionable young person during the hippie era, Jesus's mandate to love seemed so right. Many people are turned off by traditional religion, but I think those who would reject the unconditional love of Jesus are few and far between.

The years that have followed can be characterized by ongoing growth, regression, stumbles and falls, new mountaintop experiences, steps backward and steps forward. I would equate the growth process to that of peeling back layers and layers of an onion. The more layers that are peeled back, the more I recognize the need to lay something down or be changed, all the while getting closer to the heart. It is a never-ending process of becoming. I think of all of the things I have learned over the years since that "pray for me" transformation experience. Some of the profound learnings have had to do with forgiving others and forgiving myself. I am learning to love without judging others.

Many years ago on a personal Emmaus walk symbolic of when Jesus walked with the disciples along the Emmaus road yet they did not recognize him until he was gone, I recognized my need to get rid of the critical spirit in my life that was so alive and well. I am learning to recognize God's ongoing presence in nature, in people, and in quiet moments, and I pray that my "eyesight" and "hearing" will continue to improve until the day I die. It is my hope that all who see me would recognize the presence of God in me, but the reality is that this will not likely be so. Nonetheless, I will continue to "run with patience, the race that is set before me … looking unto Jesus, the author and finisher of my faith." (Hebrews 12:1–2)

After three years of seminary, my husband became a pastor. Unlike the experience of many pastors' wives, this was not necessarily a negative experience for me. There were some negatives associated with the position, but generally speaking it was a positive experience. It is often difficult, however, for the spouse and family of a pastor to have one's own personal friendships and relationships outside of the church. I once heard someone say that the life of a pastor creates neurotic people because their work environment, their social contacts, and their family relationships are often all in one place. For most people and professions, these three groups are completely separate and distinctly different. Because I was used to being alone and not having close personal friends, this may have been less difficult for me. In this role I continued to grow in my relationship with God. God was my source of strength, my best friend. I longed to be a good wife and mother, and I continued to take seriously the teachings of Jesus and their practical implications for my life.

One of my most significant experiences in the early years of my husband's ministry was my participation in a teacher/disciple program. A young single woman in our church invited me to become her mentor in this program. Rather than being a teacher/disciple team, I think we were both disciples eager to grow in our personal faith. We met weekly for a period of two years. Together we learned to do inductive Bible study: taking a passage of scripture, translating it into language that we could understand, and discussing how we could apply it to our everyday lives. The more I understood, the more I wanted to grow. We prayed together for each other and for ourselves. We shared areas of need in our lives. All that I learned in that two-year experience continues to impact my life and my Christian walk today.

You may be wondering why I have titled this chapter "The Love of My Life." Throughout my life I have compromised either my values or my feelings in an effort to meet my needs for affection, affirmation, and validation as a person of value and worth, a person created right and with purpose. In my relationships with my spouses, I never asked God for validation of the relationship. I made my choices based on my own unmet needs. I have finally learned that when I settle for less than what God has planned for me, I cannot possibly experience life to the fullest as God intended for me. There is no question about it: God will walk with us wherever we go, but our own choices often limit the quality of our life.

In my first marriage, I was unconsciously looking for a kind father, someone who would love me, take care of me, share the same values and interests, and respect who I was as a person. Even though I agreed to trade off feelings of love and affection, I didn't see why it wouldn't work. I wasn't very good at sharing intimately anyway. I now understand that the intimacy between husband and wife is critical to the marriage relationship, kind of like the glue that holds all things together.

In my second marriage, there was physical chemistry, and in the beginning my husband showered me with affection. That soon lost its glamour when he challenged my values, rejected my children, and criticized me for living out my deep Christian convictions. Although he initially told me that he had never known anyone who actually lived out Christian values and he wanted to learn and to grow, it became very clear that this was not the deep desire of his heart. I had again compromised all that was important to me for one unmet need in my life. Did I ask God whether I should do this? No. Did I want God to bless this decision? Of course. Was all that followed God's fault? Of course not! I was once again living with the consequences of my own decision and settling for far less than God intended for me.

You might ask how God can be the love of my life since I have had such need for intimacy and affection. I am continually learning more and more about how intimate my relationship with God can be, and I am sure there is much more for me to learn. There are some things I now know and will never compromise again.

I know that when God's word says "God loves you," it is forever and unconditional. God loves me just because I am. There is nothing I have to do to receive God's love other than accept it. God will never hurt me; I am safe with God. God knows the cry of my heart whether I am afraid, confused, angry, sad, or lonely. Whenever I choose to talk to God, God listens. Sometimes God disciplines me, gently showing me the dangers and consequences of my wrong choices, but always with love and tenderness, never to produce self-condemnation. There is nowhere that I can go that God will not be with me, and God has promised to give my life meaning and purpose. God has said that I am fearfully and wonderfully made (Psalm 139), so that definitely has an impact on my self-esteem, helping me to feel good about myself. God's mercies are new every morning, and the more I walk with God, the more I recognize God's presence and voice in the world around me and in the people brought into my life.

To have this kind of relationship with another human being who knows this same love relationship with God would be wonderful. But for me, I can finally say this is God's business. I will bask in God's love and provision for me today and never again compromise the values that are so dear to me.

If you struggle with some of these same issues, I know from personal experience that this same incredibly loving God can meet all of your needs as well. We are told that Jesus experienced every experience common to humankind and that if we cast our cares upon him, he is faithful to meet our every need. I wish you joy on your journey, joy that exceeds any happy moment, joy that abides deep in your heart, joy that enables you to soar like eagles above any circumstance or trial. What a gift, incredible joy, just for the asking! So now you know why I have chosen God to be the love of my life, the most treasured relationship in my life.

# Peace, Power, and Hope

Throughout the years God has spoken to me in powerful ways, assuring me of his presence to bring me peace and to offer me hope. Every person's experience is different. I want to share some of my experiences with you in hopes that it will broaden your understanding of who God is and how personal He can be. I hope it will encourage you to think about your own experience with God and recognize His incredible love and care for you. I hope that what I share will reaffirm that God will never leave you or forsake you, that He will always be there to meet your need in every situation, and that it is His greatest desire to be in communion with you.

The more I learn the teachings of God's word, take them into my heart, and apply them to my life, the more I experience God's power. There are many scriptures that are particularly meaningful to me, and I will share some of them with you.

My favorite scripture of all is found in Galatians 2:20. The Living Bible says it this way: "I have been crucified with Christ and I myself no longer live, but Christ lives in me. And the real life I now live in this body is the result of my trusting in the son of God who loved me and gave himself for me." I know that many of the detours I have taken in my life are the result of my own wrong choices. As human beings we are incapable of perfection. We make mistakes, and often our choices are the result of selfish desires or unrealistic goals. We see with tunnel vision where God sees from a panoramic view. For me, this verse tells me that by surrendering to the love of God, God's spirit dwells within me, and I no longer need to depend on my needy human nature for wisdom.

One thing is clear to me as I think about the times in my life when I know God has clearly spoken to me. They had nothing to do with spiritual maturity. They had more to do with a listening ear. I tell you this because I want you to know without question that when you cry out to God, no matter where you are on your faith journey, God does hear your cry and desires to meet your need. The more we are willing to listen for His voice, the more we learn and grow and see His presence and power at work in our lives.

As I look back on my own faith journey, I am amazed at the number of experiences that come to my mind, experiences that clearly illustrate the power of a living God to give direction and chart the course. I am overwhelmed by the fact that God is so personal, so merciful, so patient. He knows all of my wrong turns, all of my wrong choices, and yet He continues to shower me with His love and gently encourage me to continue to grow in my walk with Him. As I share these examples of peace, power, and hope, I hope that you will recognize the power of the Creator within you. If you have never heard His voice, maybe these illustrations will enable you to recognize His presence within you.

I am reminded and comforted that God used ordinary, flawed people to convey his message of love to the world, and this brings me hope. Abraham was afraid and tried to pass his wife off as his sister so that the king could take her for himself, and yet God told him that he would become the "father of nations." David committed adultery and then murder as he sent Bathsheba's husband to the front lines of battle where he knew he would be killed. And God said David was "a man after His own heart." After the crucifixion, Peter denied he ever knew Jesus, not one time but three times, and Jesus said Peter's name should be "Rock" and "on this Rock I will build my church." These examples give me hope to believe that God can love me and use me in spite of my own flaws.

In Ephesians 3:20 it is written, "Exceedingly, abundantly, above all we ask or think, that's what our God can do." Jesus said, "Peace I leave with you. My peace I give to you. I do not give to you as the world gives. Don't let your hearts be troubled and do not be afraid." Jesus and the disciples were out in a boat when a storm came up. The disciples were very afraid. Jesus was sleeping. He awakened, acknowledged their fear, and spoke to the turbulent water, saying "Peace, be still." The storm ceased, the waters calmed, and the disciples' fears were dispelled. (Matthew 8:23–27)

One of my earliest adult memories of God's presence, His power, and His peace came to me at the age of twenty-four as I experienced surgery on both sides of both feet, something very unusual for such a young woman. Prior to the surgery, I had been experiencing incredible pain. I was very much afraid of the thought of surgery, never having experienced anything other than a tonsillectomy as a young child. I asked the surgeon if the surgery would be painful. He admitted to me that surgery on joints was always painful. He told me that one side of one foot was going to "hurt like hell." And he was going to fix both sides of both feet all at the same time. Great—I could hardly wait! In the days that led up to the surgery, it seemed like the pain increased tenfold. So when the day of the surgery actually arrived, I could not wait for the pain to be over. I knew there would be pain from the surgery, but it was going to be so much better. I was no longer afraid of anesthesia and surgery and all that went with it. Before I went into surgery, my husband prayed with me in my hospital room. He prayed for healing and asked that angels would surround me and be present in my room. He asked God to be present in the surgery and to give me peace.

All went well with the surgery, and I knew ahead of time that I would be in the hospital for five days. On the day following the surgery, I was amazed that I did not have any pain. Our pastor came to visit, and he commented that there was something strangely peaceful about my room, as if he were in the presence of angels. We told him that we had prayed for God to be at work in the hands of the surgeon and that angels would surround me and be present in my room. Through the entire experience, I remained pain-free. God not only heard my prayers but provided for my healing way beyond any expectation that I might have had, even to the amazement of my doctor. What did I do to deserve such care? Nothing! This was an incredible gift of healing and peace. It was simply a gift from God, just the first of many that I would experience in the years to come.

One of the next messages that comes to mind came when my oldest son was about two years old. He was such a wonderful child, easy to care for, happy, full of energy, and never naughty. He was the greatest joy of my life. I wanted so much to have children to love and to nurture. He was such a gift, and I wanted to be the best mom anyone could be. I had no idea that I was filled with such destructive anger. I don't even remember what he did, but it must have been something that irritated me. I hauled off and swatted him on his back side, and it seemed the voice filled the room with a mighty roar: "If you continue to discipline this child in this way, he will hate you as much as you hated your own father." Whoa, where did that come from? It was the voice of a loving God who wanted to teach me how to discipline my child in a way that would be beneficial to him. The message was clear—control your anger, take a few minutes to breathe, and allow God to give you wisdom that will bring forth positive fruit in this child. Thank you, God, I never lashed out in anger at him again. This was a powerful moment of revelation for me, and I knew that God wanted to teach me a better way.

When my son was about three, a dear friend had just returned home from the hospital following complications from the birth of her fourth child. She had two three-year-olds and a two-year-old at home as well. I wanted to be helpful, so I planned the day to take my son and spend the day at her home to do whatever I could. The last thing I did before I left her house was prepare dinner for her family. In those days we were not nearly as nutrition conscious as today. I was frying chicken in about an inch of grease. The chicken had been frying for about forty-five minutes, so you can imagine that the grease was very hot. I really don't know how it happened, but as I was taking the chicken out of the grease, I turned the frying pan upside down onto my hand. I was shocked at what I had done and then began to feel the pain of the burn. I turned on the cold water, put my hand under the faucet, and prayed. "Lord, I came here to be helpful. I simply cannot be burned. I am late; I need to go home and prepare dinner for my own family, and it is a forty-five-minute drive. Please take away this pain and touch this hand." I continued to hold my hand under the faucet, and I noticed that it wasn't hurting anymore. There were a few red streaks between my fingers where the grease had run down onto the back side of my hand, but there were no blisters. By the time I returned home, most of the redness was gone. I was so grateful because my husband was not happy with me that we were late. After all, it was my responsibility to take care of my own family first. God knew that I needed his healing touch. Talk about the power of God to heal.

Have I experienced healing every time I prayed for it since then? No, but I never stop asking. It is God Himself who decides when and how to heal so that the world can know that He is in control. This incident took place more than thirty-five years ago, and it is still ever present in my mind. It is a reminder to me that God heard my prayer, knew my need, and knew that His healing power in that incident would strengthen my faith ever after.

When our son was two, we applied for a second adoption. We asked for another boy. We (or I) rationalized that it would be good for us to have another boy because we lived in a two-bedroom house. Boys could share the same room, share clothes, etc. We had a limited income, and it seemed to make financial sense that another boy would be less costly than having a girl. However, deep in my soul, I knew I was afraid of having a girl. Because I had such a poor relationship with my own mother growing up, I was afraid that I could not be a good mom to a girl.

I specifically remember asking for prayer in a small Bible study group of women with whom I met regularly. I asked for prayer for the birth mother who would carry our new unborn child. I remember one member of the group questioning why I would ask for a prayer like that. Well, God had a reason. He had prompted me to ask for prayer, and I consistently prayed for the well-being of the child and birth mother throughout the pregnancy. When you adopt, you have no way of knowing how long it will be before a child is placed with you. When the call came on a Thursday night, I answered the phone about seven. The social worker said that it was noted in our file that we might consider a girl if too much time passed between our request and the actual availability of a child. The social worker said that they had a baby girl for us if we wanted her; could we come and pick her up at nine in the morning? What a shock! A baby girl with no warning, but aha—our second incredible gift from God. God promptly reminded me that it was exactly nine months from the time I asked that small group of women to pray for the birth mother and our unborn child. I knew without question that it would be okay, that God knew my fears and He would provide a way for this mother-daughter relationship to be good.

To this day I do not know what my daughter would say, but I never questioned again that I could be a good mom to a daughter. She was then and continues to be a very special gift to me. Today she is a beautiful, loving, compassionate mother of three of my wonderful grandchildren. Talk about the power of God to impact lives—not only my life but the lives of generations to come. God is so good! This story is written in the front of her baby book as a reminder to her that God had a plan for her and for me as well.

When my daughter was fourteen months old, my husband had knee surgery that resulted in the passing of blood clots through his heart and lung. During this time a young family came to stay with our children as I went back and forth to the hospital. This was a very stressful time, as my husband's life was seriously threatened. It took several days until his blood was sufficiently thinned so that it would no longer clot. Then he hemorrhaged in his joint. All in all he was in the hospital for twenty-six days out of six weeks.

A young family from our church was so gracious to come to our house and stay with our children. As I drove into the driveway, I heard the screams of my daughter, who had just severely burned her face and the front half of her body. The father had filled a coffee cup with boiling coffee, set it on a desk, and went to get his toddler son, who was playing in the toilet. During that brief moment, my daughter, who had just taken her first steps, pulled the cup off of the desk and poured the boiling coffee onto herself. I will never forget the screams. I was grateful for a calm presence of mind. I put a cold cloth on her burned body and called the doctor, who was a member of our church and a personal friend, at his home. He told me he would need to wait for his wife to return home. He would call me back, and then I should meet him at his office.

As I waited about twenty minutes for the phone call, I prayed that God would protect and heal my precious daughter. The burns were severe—blisters gone and raw flesh everywhere. From the sound of her screams, I knew the pain must have been severe, as well. To my amazement, as I gently rocked this precious little girl in my lap and waited, my baby fell asleep.

The doctor said that it would be important for the wounds to heal from the inside out in order to prevent scarring. It would be very important that the wounds not become infected. She was bandaged from her head to her waist. She did experience some infection close to her mouth where it was very difficult to keep food from getting into the bandages. As a mixed-race child, we could expect there might be some scarring or skin discoloration. To this day no one would ever know that she had been burned. There was no scarring on her face, and the only evidence would be a slightly speckled pigmentation on her chest.

In this experience I not only witnessed the power of God to heal but to bring peace in a very difficult situation. What were the chances that my baby would fall asleep after such a traumatic experience? Again, God is good!

As I have mentioned before, I have often heard the voice of God while running. On this particular spring day, my running partner and I were running in silence on our normal route when we passed a beautiful magnolia tree. The tree was in full bloom, and I thought about what a mess it would make on the grass as the blooms fell to the ground. I didn't say anything to my running partner as we continued our run. The route took us to the end of a circle, and then we ran back the same way we had come. As we passed the tree again, the voice was so clear: "You idiot, I created such a beautiful tree and all you can think about is what a mess it will make on the ground. What is wrong with your thinking? Why not choose to focus on the beauty instead of the negative?" I shared this message with my friend. The power of that incident changed my life ever after. I no longer focus on the negative but try to see the beauty and good in every situation. The next time we ran past that tree, there was no mess on the ground. Was I asking God to speak to me in this experience? No. I guess He just took a chance that I might hear his voice. I am so glad I did. Life is so much easier when I choose to focus on the positive.

Our children have a very special place in our hearts, and we would do anything for them. Our hearts are tender as we ask God for wisdom to nurture and train them in His ways. In the experience with learning to control my anger with my young son, God was speaking to me about how to be a good mom and to discipline with love. This next experience again involves my daughter. It is not about discipline, but it is about crying out to God for the best for her. I don't think there has been any other experience in my life that has had such a profound impact on me. It is about trusting God, knowing that He is in control and that I can rest in His care even when I cannot see the outcome. It reminds me that faith is about believing what I cannot see.

As is often the case, I seem to be more receptive to hear the voice of God when I am running. It is quiet; I am alone with God and not distracted. I see Him in the beauty of His creation, and I am keenly aware of His presence.

It was very early in the morning; the sun had not risen, and the moon was big and bright, around five in the morning. I was running down the hill and came to a bridge over a small creek. The water in front of me was illuminated by the moon, and then the creek curved, and it was very dark beyond where the light of the moon was shining on the water. I was crying out to God, "Lord, Lord, what if she can't read?" My daughter was in first grade and showed no indication that she was learning to read. I was concerned that she was going to have serious learning problems. She was a very quiet and shy child, and very strong-willed at times. I didn't expect my children would be rocket scientists, but I had at least hoped they would have average abilities and grow to be responsible, caring adults.

The message was so unbelievably clear, you know, kind of like that "you idiot" message. "I did not give this child to you to teach her how to read. I gave her to you to love. So why don't you let my light shine on you, just like the moonlight on the water in front of you, to be the best possible influence on her *today* and then let me take care of what is around the corner that you cannot see and cannot control?" Wow! Again, through nature, God had spoken a powerful message to me. It was a message of power, of peace and of hope, all in one.

To my great surprise, the answer to my question was also clear. That week was open house at school. My daughter took me to her classroom, showed me her desk, and pulled out a book which she proceeded to read to me. I picked her up and twirled her around. She might have thought I was nuts because she had no idea what was going on in my head. Of course, she knew nothing about my heart-to-heart with God about her ability to read. Again and again and again, God is so good!

When we are walking closely with God and are obedient to His word, we can expect that He will reveal himself to us in meaningful ways. I was feeling particularly close to God and leading a very special group of wounded women who were learning to trust in God for healing in their lives. We met weekly in a local church, and often I would prepare for the meeting early in the morning before going to work. On this particular morning, I wrote down what seemed like a monologue from God that I felt He wanted me to share with my dear friends. It was a message of encouragement about His profound love for each one of them. I could hardly write fast enough as the message came. It was so clear that God was speaking, and I was excited about sharing His message with this group of women who seemed to be so receptive to hear His voice.

We were meeting in a small room on the first floor, directly beneath the sanctuary. The church was hosting a national conference that week, and as we met for our weekly meeting, the conference worship service was convened upstairs. Just as I came to the part in this intimate conversation with God where God said, "Listen, can you not hear the angels singing?" the room was filled with the sound of an angelic choir from upstairs. I still get goose bumps as I think about this today. Not only did God give me the message to share with my friends, He was preparing that angelic choir to burst forth in praise at just the right moment, all for the purpose of showing us how loving and how powerful He is. The group wept with joy at the power of His presence in that room that night.

Have you ever been beside yourself, not knowing which way to turn, feeling like there is no hope and no way out? I mean at rock bottom, really afraid and alone, not being able to see how you can go on. I am guessing more of us have been there than we will ever know. I won't go into detail, but will just say that this was one of the lowest moments in my life. I was a strong person and had endured a lot, but this incident was both emotionally and financially devastating to me. When I finally was able to sleep, God appeared to me in a dream. How did I know it was a dream from God? The message was clear, and it brought me hope—hope to go on, one step at a time, moving forward and trusting that He was there, knew the situation, and He *would* take care of me. That dream occurred more than twenty years ago, and today I am living proof of its powerful impact. It was significant in healing my hurt, enabling me to forgive, and once again reminding me that He would never leave me or forsake me. I remember my mother saying to me during that time, "There is always a way." Imagine that, God using my own mother to encourage me and give me hope. She was right, and the dream confirmed her message.

The dream went like this. I arrived home one night, and I could not get into my house. Although I had a key, it did not work on any of the doors. Everything I owned that was important to me was in that house. It was my place of refuge, of peace and safety. I was locked out and had nowhere to go for help. I was alone and afraid and desperate. It all seemed so impossible. I just crumpled up in a pile outside the door, crying out, "What will I do?" And then the voice came: "Be not afraid. The doors are not the only way into this house. Yes, the doors are locked, and you cannot enter the same way. Things are changing, and you will need to adjust, but you can get in. It is your home, and you will survive. I am with you, and I will make a way." You may have heard it said that when God closes a door He opens a window. I don't necessarily believe that it was God who locked the door, but I do believe that he opened the window. In the dream I was finally able, with some effort, to get in through a window, and there was a glimmer of hope that I would be okay. If you have ever been or are in that dark scary place, I pray that you too will call out to the Father of Life for His healing, His protection, and His care. He *will* hear your prayer and heal your heart!

The last experience I want to share with you is very recent. After all of these years on this journey of faith, I think I am finally getting it that the goodness of God's way will always be beyond any earthly expectation. Don't you think it is about time, after sixty-five years on this earth? I said earlier that my son gave me a mug on my sixtieth birthday that said, "Finally, getting a handle on life." And my response was that I was looking forward to the next thirty years of living as a whole person. This experience was probably the biggest step of faith I have ever taken. I sure wish I had prayed about my marriages as much as I prayed about this. Surely the outcome would have been much different. Better late than never!

As I awoke from a nap one day in my recliner in the living room of my very lovely home, it was like a light bulb turned on in my head. The message was clear: "If you would sell this house, downsize, and move, you could be mortgage-free going into retirement!" I was reminded that what makes a home special is not the physical structure but the creative energy put into it to make it a place of peace and warmth. Those attributes could be created in other places. I loved this house. I spent nineteen years tenderly maintaining it, updating it, using my creative imagination to make it the perfect place of peace and tranquility. Yes, it was a lot of work to keep it up, but it was so rewarding. People loved to come here. Both inside and out, it was a peaceful place where people felt welcome and comfortable. I shared it often with many people. It was God's gift entrusted to me to share with others, and I liked that.

As much as I loved the house, the idea of being debt-free going into retirement was particularly appealing to me. Much of my adult life I struggled with the need to make ends meet to simply survive. I had become a very good manager. I know some would call that being tight to a fault. The fear inside of me of not having enough money to survive was not nearly as powerful as it had once been. However, the closer I got to retirement, the more I knew that I would need to plan carefully for my future, since I was the only one on this earth who was going to take care of me. Yes, God would be present with me, but He would also expect me to be responsible and wise with all that He had entrusted to me. We are really only stewards of all that He has given us.

Rather unemotionally I said, "Okay, God, but you know how important it is to me to walk to work. I am going to drive around the block and see if any houses are for sale." Much to my surprise, there was an interesting house just around the corner with a For Sale sign in the yard. It was just about the same distance from work as my current house, in a much less expensive but acceptable neighborhood. There were no gaslights in every yard, and the mailboxes were not all the same. There were a few more dandelions, but people seemed to take care of their yards and take pride in their homes.

After work I called the realtor listed on the sign and asked to see the home. Again, much to my surprise, the home was owned by the construction and turnover supervisor at my work. I knew that he had a house for sale on this street, but I did not know that it was so close to work. He had made many lovely improvements in the home and was eager to sell the house as he had purchased another property in the country with more space for his young family.

I had checked with my financial advisor about the wisdom of selling my home, downsizing, getting rid of my mortgage, purchasing another home, and coming out with no debt, even after making changes to a new property. He had told me that if I could come out even, it would be a great idea.

So I prayed. "God, if this is what you want me to do, then give me green lights along the way. If not, show me big red flags so that I know which way to go." The green lights kept coming at every turn, and I recognized God's leading. I was finally trusting God's leading with all my heart. With the equity in my current home, I was able to get a line of credit to pay off my mortgage. I stepped out in faith and made an offer on the new house. The offer was accepted, and I put my lovely home up for sale.

Economic times were difficult, and we had just come out of a recession. Houses were for sale everywhere, and it was a buyers' market. In my particular more upscale neighborhood, houses were not moving at all, and owners were being forced to reduce the prices again and again. I knew how much I needed for my house in order to pay off the mortgage and make changes in the new house. I could hardly believe that I, who had been forever afraid of financial risk, committed to the purchase of another property before my home was sold. Nothing but the power of God could make that happen. I waited patiently for a period of six months, never wavering that this was God's leading.

Was I crazy taking on a hefty line of credit payment, two utility bills, insurance payments, and taxes on two properties in a market when houses were not selling? No, I was not nuts, I was simply, finally allowing God to lead my decision-making process and provide the way financially for my future. It was a step of faith like I had never taken before. Even the realtor commented that she was amazed that I was not thrown into panic mode and reducing the price just to get rid of the debt.

Did the house sell? Of course it did, to some very special friends who were seeking God's will for their own situation. They cared very much about being fair and knew what I needed for my house. They were thrilled with my home and felt it was clearly an answer to their prayers. Lesson learned: When you step out in faith and follow God's leading, He is faithful to provide "exceedingly, abundantly, above all we ask or think."

I am amazed as I share these experiences with you at the ways God has so clearly spoken to me over the years. When I put them down on paper, it may seem as though God and I were always in close communion. Remember, all of these events occurred over a period of forty years, and there were plenty of times when I neither asked God to speak to me nor sought His wisdom. I did not always make the right choices and often had to live with the consequences of those wrong choices. But there is no question, as I reflect on this long journey, that God is incredibly patient and ever loving, and He longs to be in communion with me. He has blessed me beyond measure and has become my very closest friend in all the world.

Paul writes in chapter one of Philippians, "My prayer for you is that you will overflow more and more with love for others, and at the same time keep on growing in spiritual knowledge and insight." And in Colossians, Paul says that he is asking that the way you live will always please the Lord and honor Him so that you will always be doing good, kind things for others, while all the time you are learning to know God better and better. I too pray that as you reflect on your life, you will recognize God's ever-present love for you and that you will hear His voice in the experiences of your life. I pray that you will desire to learn and grow in His way and that you will be free to become all that God intended you to be. Because, after all, becoming is what it is all about. Hopefully you will come to this place in your life *before* you turn sixty! I wish you blessings and peace.

# Poetic Gifts of Inspiration

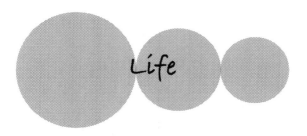

Life

Be not afraid,
Stand firm,
Rooted and secure,
Steadfast in the love of the Father,
Equipped for all that is to come.

Reflections

The wonder of creation makes its presence known
From the heights of the heavens to the depths of the sea.
The beauty of the earth is all around us.

Can it be possible that anything can surpass such splendor?

Only when one experiences the depth of human caring, the unconditional love of another, the never-ending love of the Father, can the beauty of creation become complete.

Is it any wonder that the Father looked upon His handiwork and pronounced it good?

May the focus of our being be upon that which is everlasting, and may our hearts be forever filled with gratitude.

# Unconditional

*Love* is a gift,
A statement of the heart,
Motivated by the One who is love.
*Love* is ever-present in the wonder of creation,
In the depths of human relationships,
In the inseparable bond between the Creator and His children.

*Love* enables;
Seeks the best for others;
Is patient;
Is kind;
Does not give up but believes;
Brings peace to troubled waters.

*Love* is forever,
A never-ending cycle of giving and receiving,
A shelter from the storm,
The source of unspeakable joy,
*a gift to be treasured.*

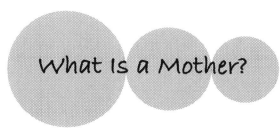

# What Is a Mother?

A vessel created to bring forth life;
An earthly example
Of love,
Of comfort,
Of safety,
Of tenderness.
But how can I in my humanness? Such an awesome task!
Then the awesome reminder comes …
I have been equipped and empowered by the Creator of life.
Walk in His way
Teach His truths
Rest in His care
And allow the beauty of creation to unfold.

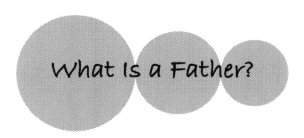

# What Is a Father?

A vessel entrusted with responsibility;
An earthly example
Of love,
Of leadership,
Of compassion,
Of strength.
But how can I in my humanness? Such an awesome task!
And then I am reminded …
I have been equipped and empowered by the Father of life.
Walk in His way,
Rely on His strength,
Rest in His care,
And allow the beauty of creation to unfold.

# Matters of the Heart

Matters of the heart are deep,
Nestled in the center of one's being
Impacting life in powerful ways,
Like the rushing stream
That flows over rock and stone,
Cleansing and purifying all in its path.

So, too, it is with matters of the heart.
When hearts are transformed,
Life bursts forth with meaning.
Love flows freely onto others,
And safety and security abound.

When love abides deep within,
The power of giving is unleashed.
When that deep abiding love is shared with another,
Purity, goodness, and affirmation
Empower that person to become.

Love is about giving, not getting.
It's about being set free from self to care about others.
It's about soaring like eagles above the cares of this world.
It's about becoming:
free and safe and at peace.

After all, becoming is what it's all about.

Printed in the United States
By Bookmasters